PYROG

A Beginner's Guide to Learning Wood Burning Techniques and Patterns

By Jeff Stanley

circumstances is the author responsible for any losses, direct or indirect, which are incurred as a result of the use of information contained within this document, including, but not limited to, — errors, omissions, or inaccuracies.

Table of Contents

INTRODUCTION

Pyrography is an art form dating back to the Seventeenth Century, although simpler forms have been practiced for much longer. It is not a commonly known or widespread art, making its use more valued and the resultant works far more sought after. You may have been introduced to it by seeing some astonishing works done by professionals on various interest pages on the internet. One of the most important bits of advice that will serve you going into this book is to keep in mind that, as with any true art, it requires practice.

There are, as with any medium in art, a near-infinite number of applications and methods by which pyrography can be utilized. While contemporary practice usually involves specialized tools, there are applications by which even magnifying glasses are used.

We know, by studying the historical background, that heated metal rods were frequently used. There is also a boundary between the more sophisticated pyrography artform and the still-fascinating, but slightly more mundane practice, referred to as 'pokerwork.'

By using various tools and different tooltips and temperatures, the pyrography artist develops a spectrum of tones and styles. This is similar to the way that other artists work by using pencils of varying weight, or inks of different consistency and opacity to create a variety of tones.

The name 'pyrography' originates from Greek, although the more simplified practice of pokerwork was practiced in Ancient Egypt, as well as among early African tribes. There is a continuous record of forms of pyrographic art existing in some capacity throughout all of recorded human history.

The modern complexities and levels of detail of modern pyrography far exceed their historical counterparts in terms of comparative quality, but it is interesting how it has played such a consistent role in human history. Yet, it is also a somewhat neglected art form when compared to more ubiquitous practices like oil painting or charcoal sketching. Perhaps this can be attributed to a general level of ignorance regarding the level of detail and artistic flexibility pyrographic art offers. Still, it is quite possible to learn it. Pyrography is sometimes offered as a short course as part of a fine art degree by colleges.

Across the world, there are communities where it is a matter of cultural pride for children to learn the art from their parents; this is a good example of cultural transmission. But, aside from courses including it, and communities that still embrace it, pyrography isn't really an art that has saturated the market.

This may sound a bit of a negative attribute, but, in the world of art, value is almost exclusively defined by demand. Consider that the fewer paintings a celebrated artist has painted, the more valuable each is considered, and the more exotic the art form, the more attention it enjoys.

This is one reason you may have your heart set on learning the plethora of skills involved. Another may be merely for the joy of expanding your creative horizons. You may think to add a *craftsy* skill to other hobbies that someone with a creative predisposition may possess.

This is a wonderful reason to explore the world of pyrography. However, as this book will suggest to you, it is well worth exploring the many facets of pyrography. It is an art that might easily be the foundation for an entire calling.

Whatever your reason and however your interest may have been piqued, this book is intended to serve as the ideal starting point for anyone hoping to enrich their lives with this intriguing and rewarding craft.

CHAPTER ONE

THE HISTORY AND ORIGINS OF PYROGRAPHY

Pyrography is a free-hand art form. The word, pyrography, is derived from two words, "pyro", meaning fire, and "graphy", which can mean "writing", "drawing", "art", or "science." The two joined words "pyrography" define the art of "writing with fire." The art, as we know it now, dates back to the 1600s, but has gained popularity with the emergence of modern pyrography tools.

There are five major parts of the skill. The tools, especially the wood burning unit. The pen tips and the skill in using them. The wood - it's selection and suitability to your intention and hoped-for results. The art work, where to find it and how to transfer it to your wood medium. Finally, your art style, your wood burning technique, and your proficiency in both. {*} *Reference: definition of pyrography*

The art has its roots in the earliest days of our shared history. The discovery of fire, or more accurately, the discovery of man's ability to manipulate fire, was the catalyst for our ancestors' creativity and desire to document their lives.

According to archaeological data, it would seem that shortly after early man discovered that the charred remains of burnt wood - the charcoal - could be used as a medium to inscribe images on the walls of their rocky cave settlements, they made the first leap to using the effects of fire to create an illustrated record.

They started scratching away at the charred sides of logs of wood that were not fully incinerated and created some of the earliest known relief art. This form of artistic expression suffered from the impermanence of its medium. There was only so long that any art created in this way could last.

As humanity continued to progress, so too did the tools available to them. It remains a fascinating field of study in the realm of anthropology. And it shows that throughout all of human history, our creativity would make use of any new technological developments.

Development of Metals as Pyrography Tools

The next step in this development may not seem quite so striking to a modern person, but the advent of manipulating metals, and the most basic qualities that these metals had, is probably one of the defining moments in all of human development.

An offshoot of this development was the ability of metals to be heated. They could maintain much higher temperatures than the silicate-based rocks that had made up most of humanity's tools until this time. The heated metals were used to inscribe imagery on to a variety of substrates. These included leather, bone, and, of course, wood. It's fascinating to note that the tradition spans the scope of ancient civilization, suggesting a profound common ancestry passed down from the age of tribal man, or, perhaps, the reinvention of the craft many times over the course of history.

The Egyptians were fond of the practice and it was the pastime of wealthy artisans. The results of their labor were prized as luxury items by the upper tier of their civilization. The Egyptians also notably combined the art form with more traditional woodwork, creating a unique blend of the two crafts. It resulted in bespoke objects often used as decor.

The ancient Peruvians were equally enamored with the practice. The Nazca and Moche civilizations of Peru were two of the more prominent groups who both used these techniques in their art. They had a fondness for what one might call wood engraving today. However, it was used on a myriad of items such as drinking cups and ceremonial bowls.

PYROGRAPHY

Anyone familiar with the history of the ancient Peruvian civilizations may not be surprised to learn that these were items often designated for ceremonial use in a religious context. There may be some correlation between the appeasement of the engraved deities and the religious enactment involved.

The Han Dynasty in China referred to the art as 'fire needle embroidery,' and there is perhaps a closer correlation between their artwork and modern pyrography. Chinese history is known for art that reflects an attention to detail, and usually the use of very delicate substrates, and this is true of the *fire needle embroidery* we see from this time.

The next step in the evolution towards modern pyrography came in the medieval era. In this time, metalworking was becoming ever more refined, leading to the invention of pokers not too different, in concept at least, to modern pens. Artisans used another new invention of the time, the portable stove. These portable stoves had holes in their lids that facilitated heating a number of pokers simultaneously. Artisans would carry a number of pokers with them because the tools quickly cooled during use. They would cycle through a process of heating cooled pokers to maintain a constant workflow.

Although these pokers were certainly the preferred tools of the trade, many other metal objects were used, including needles and knives. To a small but significant degree, the art form had become more accessible. It is now thought that blacksmiths commonly enjoyed the craft as a hobby, as they had all the equipment needed. Furthermore, it is possible that many blacksmiths subsidized their income by selling the products of their dabbling.

At this time, the art form had, as mentioned, started to resemble the modern art of pyrography more closely than ever before, but it lacked the nuanced detail and precision that defines modern artistic renditions done by a skilled master.

The 1900s provided an invention that would change the way artists could engage with this practice forever. In Melbourne, an architect by the name of Alfred Smart discovered that he could keep a new form of poker, essentially a sort of pencil-like object, heated indefinitely.

By running benzine through a solid platinum 'pencil' and using a rubber ball mechanism to keep the flow, he could maintain a heated tip. This was the missing ingredient to the evolution of pyrography, as this new technique allowed for variation in the burning process.

These variations came in the form of shading and tinting, both artistic skills that had as yet been unavailable to the avid 'pokerworker.' Finally, pyrography could assume its place as an acknowledged art form diverse enough in its application to rival any discipline in the world of creative media.

Gender Inclusion in Modern Pyrography

As with so many vocations and art forms throughout history, pyrography remained predominantly in the hands of male practitioners. This changed shortly after the invention of these new tools, albeit not necessarily for the progressive reasons one might have hoped! Housewives were handed these new machines because they were expected to decorate their homes. Women had traditionally done needlework and similar domestic arts; perhaps this was seen as an extension of that. The trend took off. It was popularized by newspapers as a respectable pastime for young ladies. This is where a small but historically significant aspect of the history of pyrography comes into play. While meant as a pastime and expected to supply home decoration, it soon offered some small level of financial impetus to women.

Constrained at the time to be entirely financially dependent and subservient, women of the time realized they could craft items to be sold to other women who had a more comfortable financial standing. This allowed the women in question to make and spend their own money, independently, although almost certainly secretly from society as a whole.

In the decades that followed, as change in social, political and technological standards began to steer humanity towards the present era, pyrography and the people that adopted it continued to veer and shift.

Nowadays, pyrography is no longer thought to be a uniquely feminine or masculine tradition; rather, it now more earnestly holds its own place in the pantheon of credible artistic disciplines.

Types of Materials Used in Pyrography

The most popular medium used for pyrography is wood. This has earned the art the more common term, "wood burning." In its earlier forms, pyrography artists used pokers which earned the art the name "poker burning." Using fire as a pen can be used on different base materials to produce beautiful works of art.

Pyrography on Leather

Pyrography will produce beautiful designs on leather. A word of caution though. Leather will burn, and it will serve you well to read up on safety before attempting to burn leather. Pyrography designs can be used on many personal items such as handbags, purses, wallets, belts, folders, and key holders.

Pyrography on Canvas

Canvas is a sturdy fabric mostly made out of cotton and PVC. It is commonly used in items made for outdoor use such as tents and bags because it's water-resistant. Decorating a bag using wood burning tools is an excellent way to use your creativity.

The materials used in making canvas make using the wood burning tool on it rather smoky and smelly. Be sure to have your safety gear on to avoid inhaling the fumes. It is also recommended that you work in a well-ventilated space.

Lower temperatures on your wood burning tool tend to work better on canvas. They will give you a smoother finish to the line work. You may increase the temperatures on your tool if you want to achieve a darker hue, but the test in control is well-worth the practice.

Pyrography on Animal Parts Such as Bone and Antlers

Hard animal parts, specifically bone and antlers, are great items to add to your collection of materials to practice your wood burning skill. Both antlers and bone are hard to burn. They will need high heat to transfer the design on to the medium. The choice of pen you will use will make a great difference in the amount of time it will take you to get the desired effect.

Pyrography on Gourds

Gourds have a hard, smooth shell making them a wonderful surface to apply wood burning images. The best pen for burning a gourd is one that allows you to regulate the temperature with ease. The gourd responds well to heat and you want to be able to regulate the temperature quickly.

The best part of using a gourd as a wood burning medium is the gourd comes with its unique dark and light patches. These will change your designs and enhance the uniqueness of each piece of art. Some of the most unique artworks will find a home on a gourd to create a spectacular finished product.

Gourds are easy to mark with a regular pencil. This makes them an easy medium to transfer your design on to. There is virtually no limit to the kind of designs you can come up with on a gourd.

Pyrography on Cork

Cork is a common material, especially in coasters. You can use your wood burning skills to turn the boring plain coaster into a finely-designed piece. The finished pieces will also make delightful gift items. Cork will require less pressure when working on it, and also a pen that will not heat too high. The advantage of designs burnt on cork is that if the coaster is used for hot dishes, the design does not peel off as it would if done in paint. The cork coaster will retain the look after use.

The granulated design of the cork may make it a bit harder to see the design before you start burning it. Wood burning stencils will help you get the perfect classy design that is both quick and simple to trace and burn-in.

Riskier Materials

Other much riskier materials used in pyrography are cotton fabrics and paper. We do not recommend these for beginners as they require extensive safety precautions. As you get better at the art, you may try your hand at these too. However, this book will focus on the most commonly used pyrography medium - wood.

Chapter Summary

- In this introductory chapter, we have traced the development of pyrography from man's discovery of fire, through to his working with metals. We saw that the early, crude forms of pyrography were called poker work. This chapter traces the development of poker work through various civilizations from Egypt, through Peru, and then to China.

- We have traced it through the 1900s to the development of the platinum pencil, to shading and tinting, and finally to the development of poker work. It is an intriguing subject to follow. Included are highlights of the different materials currently used in pyrography art, such as leather, canvas, bones, gourds, and others.

- Finally, we've looked at the modern art and its definitions. We've indicated that the most common form of pyrography is called wood burning.

In the next chapter, we will look at:

- Pyrography tools and other supplies.

CHAPTER TWO

PYROGRAPHY TOOLS AND OTHER SUPPLIES

Pens and tips! Two terms that are used interchangeably in pyrography, although they do not mean the same thing. Before you go shopping for pyrography supplies, let's get some common errors out of the way by discussing what you should know about the various burning tools available in the market and the supplies that are important to the art.

Pyrography Wood Burning Unit

The pyrography unit refers to the technology of the pyrography pen and how it connects to electricity. There are three major ways the pyrography pen will transmit electrical current.

The single temperature pyrography pen

PYROGRAPHY

The first is a one temperature tool. Once you fit the unit to the electrical outlet, it will build up to a constant temperature. Some people may refer to this pen as a soldering iron. This is accurate to an extent. The soldering iron can, in fact, be used quite effectively in pyrography. However, the pyrography tool tends to be smaller than the actual soldering iron.

A pyrography pen looks much like a soldering iron

The Rheostat and Other Pyrography Pens

The second is a rheostat pyrography pen. From the name, you get the same sense as the thermostat, which means the unit heats and cools without the user necessarily having to switch it off. The unit may come with a temperature control toggle-button; that will help you regulate the heat. The third pyrography pen looks much like the rheostat pen.

It has temperature control inbuilt in the control panel and has a temperature control dial. By turning the knob, you increase or decrease the temperature. This is the pyrography pen that comes as the highest recommended for beginners. It may, however, be a bit costlier than the simple pyrography pen without temperature control.

The rheostat pyrography pen will have a temperature control unit

Your choice of and cost of equipment will be determined by the reason you have for going into pyrography. If it is a simple hobby, you might choose to pick the one temperature tool. They tend to be cheaper. If you want to take your skill to a higher level, maybe even an income-generating art, a temperature control unit is highly recommended.

Wood Burning Tips and Pens

The most fundamental wood burning tool will be your pyrography pen, also called a wood burning pen. The pyrography pen will attach to an electrical outlet on one end, have the control unit in the middle, and have a pen tip at the other end.

The burner has an element within it and will transfer the heat to the tip once the unit is attached to the electrical outlet. For most pens, the pen holder will have a heat-resistant handle. The more sophisticated pyrography pen is larger and has a bulkier feel to it. The most common pen and the one we recommend for the beginner feels closer to the ordinary pen.

Some products on the market will have more than one burner in a unit. The choice between a unit with a single burner or one with multiple-burners will be up to you. Some artists find the ability to change burners useful.

As one moves to developing more detailed work, it helps to have at least two pen tips available as you work.

The pen tip may be long or short, a factor that will significantly affect how the pen handles. When starting on a budget, you may choose to start with a pen with a fixed tip. For a few more bucks up to the high-end range, you will get burners that are separate from the pen tips.

Pens with separate pen tips will give you a wider range of burn potential and will serve you as your art becomes more complex and detailed. This is because you get pen tips that can do more and produce more versatile lines, shapes, and designs. You will learn more about this as we continue.

In this chapter, we will discuss pens, pen tips, accessories, and supplies that are important for your art.

Pyrography Pen tips

Pyrography pen tips are in three basic categories; writers, skews, and shaders. We will get into the details of each much later. The only exception in pyrography kits are the stamps which are manufacturer-specific and can be used for creative designs.

Each pen tip, as we will see when we get to it, serves a different purpose. It produces a distinctly different line on the medium. The 'skews' have a thin crisp line, the 'writers' a wider and softer line, the 'shaders' cover a broader area.

The wire-tip writer

By the end of this book, or sooner, we hope you will
be able to conceptualize the image you have and what you
want to achieve. With the knowledge from the book, you

will be able to identify the pen tip you will use to achieve that artistic result you want and the best pen tip for it.

Pyrography Pens or Wood Burning Pens

Wood burning pens are classified into two main types and identified by the pen tips. The "solid point" and the "wire nib" pyrography pen.

1. Solid-point pyrography pen

The pyrography solid-point wood burner.

As the name suggests, the solid-point pen will have a... sorry... solid point. You will see the difference as soon as you get to the next one, I promise! They are made from brass most of the time. The solid-point pens tend to have a fixed temperature. They are, therefore, preferred for the beginner pyrography artist. They allow the artist to keep a steady pace without having to pause and wait for the temperature to stabilize.

2. Wire-nib pyrography pen

The wire-nib pen has a thin metal tip that runs across the top of the pen. The wire comes in varying sizes or gauges to create a wider burn with a thicker wire or a narrower burn if the wire is thinner. Generally speaking, experts suggest that wire nib pens allow for more burning options. This should not be taken to be an idea cast in stone, though.

The solid-tip pen can do everything the wire-tip can do. What it boils down to is the proficiency of the user. It may take you a bit more practice to achieve the same results with a solid-tip as you do with a wire-tip, but when all is said and done, you will eventually choose what works for you.

Factors to Consider When Buying Your First Pen

You do not need to remember everything in this section at first glance. But I'd suggest you mark the page;

you can always come back to it when you are ready to go pen shopping.

Wood burning pens will additionally have one of two variables: a fixed pen tip or replaceable pen tip. The difference is precisely as the description says. The fixed pen tip is not removable. The burner with replaceable pen tips comes with a set of pen tips. The range of the pen tips in the pack is determined by the manufacturer.

Generally speaking, the fixed pen tips have a more secure connection to the electrical circuit. They also provide a steady heat output. They do cost more. The set may have one or more burners, mostly two. The fixed pen tip is the upgrade from the soldering iron. As a result of that little bit of history, you will find that there are two sizes. One is preferred by seasoned pyrographers who do bulk work. It is bulkier, clumsier to handle until you get the hang of it, and more difficult to store. There is also an edition that is preferred by most artists. It is a bit smaller and thus easier to handle.

The replaceable pen tip has the same soldering iron concept, but the tips come separately. This allows the buyer to decide how much they want to spend on pen tips. The downside in use is you have to completely switch off the burner to change your pen tip.

In addition to all that's just been said, here is a list of points to remember that will help you make the best-considered choice when buying your first pen.

- *Identify how the pen tips attach to the pen.*

Pens with detachable pen tips will employ different technologies to keep the tip firmly in place. They may be screw-on, snap-on, etc. You can have fun with this and choose an attachment style that suits your personality.

You will need to remember how your tips attach to your pen. When you are going in for a new set of tips, always confirm that the new ones will attach in the same way as your existing tips unless you are buying the whole unit.

- *Know what metal is used on the tip.*

Brass will heat faster and retain heat longer. It will become soft when hot. Before you learn how to use just the right pressure for your tip, you could bend a number of tips.

- *How comfortable is the pen in your hand*

Just as a regular pen, the pyrography pen should be comfortable in your grip. With practice, you will get the hang of it, but here are some basic guidelines. If the tip is too short, then your fingers will be too near the hot tip. This could make you uncomfortable. If the tip is too long, then it will be more difficult to control the pen tip. Choose a length that feels comfortable for you. You also want to test the weight of the pen. Some might feel too heavy for your hand, and others just right. If it is too heavy, it will slow you down as you will need to rest your hand too often as you work.

- *Find out how the temperature control adjusts the heat*

Since wood burning is about burning, find out how the temperature control of the pen works. A great pen gives you constant temperature. It will also give you a temperature control console that will enable you to adjust your heat based on the effect you want to produce. You may also want to find out how fast it heats. Those seconds, whether waiting for the tip to heat or to cool, add up in time.

- *Balance the number of tips you pick up.*

There is such a thing as buying tips that are too few and tips that are too many. Too few, and your pen will not do what you want it to do; you will run short of options. Too many, and you will get overwhelmed. Keep a nice range at the beginning at around ten on the higher side. You want to make sure in your first set of pen tips you have at least two of a writer, a shader, and a skew tip.

- *Know how the pen rests when not in use*

Some units come with a housing for the hot pen. If you have that, then all you need to do is develop a habit of placing the pen back in its housing any time you're not using it. If your pen does not have a housing, make sure you pick one that rests with the pen tip facing upwards.

- *What additions does the kit have*

Some kits will come with carbon papers, patterns, stencils, and even colored pencils. These are a lovely addition to your range of tools and will give you more variety as you develop your art. Some kits will come with a tool bag or a storage box. That's great for when you want to move your work to another site or are traveling.

Pen Handling

- Do not bend the tip when removing it from the pen.

- Avoid removing the tip when it is hot. Hot metal is easier to damage.

- Do not use your tips to burn other metals. This may damage the tip.

- Always clean your tips when they are cold.

Other Wood Burning Supplies

The use of the items listed here will become clearer when we get to discussing techniques of wood burning. This is a brief list.

Designs

Where can you get ideas or designs for your wood burning project?

If you can draw your own designs, that is an excellent place to start. You can also get tons of websites that offer free wood burning designs. They range from the simpler word and line designs to the more complicated animal and landscape designs. You will choose the design according to your skill level. You may also find books that are dedicated to providing design ideas. Always check the copyright terms if you intend to sell your completed art.

Pencils

To transfer your art or design to the wood media, you will need pencils. Pencils come in two types; graphite pencils and charcoal pencils. Graphite pencils are the ordinary pencils. Charcoal pencils write darker and have a softer writing core. Pick a set of each; you will always use pencils at one point or other. We will discuss their specific use later in the book.

Transfer Papers

Graphite paper, also called transfer paper, is a good addition to your list of supplies. Carbon paper is useful too, but if you can get graphite paper, you can pass on the carbon paper. This will be used to trace your design. We will discuss that in detail later under design transfer methods.

Sandpaper

Know your sandpaper because, in wood burning, you will work with sandpaper often. Sandpaper is graded from coarse to super-fine. Coarse is graded as 40 to 60 grit. Medium at 80 to 120 grit. Fine at 150 to 180 grit. Very fine at 220 to 240 grit. Extra fine at 280 to 320 grit. Super fine is the smoothest and graded at 360 grit and above.

The sandpaper grade you will use is determined by the quality of your piece of wood. Smoothing the surface of your wood will make it easier to draw on. Rough grooves will make it extra-difficult to work with your pyrography pen. You move from the lower grit sandpaper to the higher grit sandpaper to get a smooth finish on your surface.

Tape

Adhesive tape is used to tape down your design. An important consideration for wood burning is tape with a lower adhesive rating. It will lift off the wood easily without leaving blotches on the wood. Low adhesive tape can also be used when transferring your design to your wood using stencils. Another type of tape that you can add to your list of purchases is heat-resistant tape. You may not use it often, but it will come in handy if you want to block off a segment of your wood.

Eye Goggles

Eye goggles will be great when you are sanding wood. The fine dust can be irritating on the eyes. You want to pick goggles that have foam padding as that will prevent the fine dust from getting to your eyes. If you do wear specs, you want to choose goggles that will fit on top of your specs.

Face Mask

Although not a necessary accessory to wear all the time, it is good to be in possession of a face mask that can filter dust and smoke. It will come in handy when you need to sand your wood or burn a segment that will char.

Wood burning will produce some smoke. We will get into that when discussing the type of wood you choose. It's highly recommended that you work in a well-ventilated space. Inhaling smoke as you work on your piece is not going to serve your health.

Heat-Resistant Gloves

A sturdy pair of heat-resistant gloves will be a great addition. They will protect your fingers when you are burning your design.

Ear Plugs

If you will sand your wood often, then add a pair of earplugs to your list of purchases.

Pure Cotton Cloth

A towel, a pure cotton cloth, or material that has some rubber underneath and cotton on top is an excellent piece to add to your list of wood burning accessories. It will be useful when sanding your wood.

Sandpaper Holder

There is a wide range of holders for sandpaper. These range from the really simple pencil-like holders to the more exotic sanders with a variety of handles. You will need sandpaper and you will need to sand your wood. So do invest in a good holder to make your work more efficient.

An Electric Wood Sander

An electric wood sander will only be a critical item to purchase if you are taking your art to a new level of commitment. But if you are working on wood burning as a hobby and for simple personal crafts, then an electric sander might be overkill. A wood sander comes in handy on larger surfaces. There are four main types of wood sanders: the random orbital sander, disc sander, the belt sander, and the finishing sander. The most common is the random orbital sander and it will serve you quite well.

Design Enhancement Items

Special pyrography paper, stencils, and other design development enhancers will make your art more fun and give you a wider range of ideas of things you can do with your piece of wood.

Chapter Summary

- The most important tool in pyrography is the wood burner. It is also referred to as the wood burning pen. In this chapter, we have described the various wood burning pens available on the market. We have also touched on the way pens are defined so that you will know how to identify the terms in the market.

- The chapter goes through the various ten tips and their main characteristics. We have also provided the reader guidelines on important aspects of wood burning pens to be aware of when buying their first wood burning kit. We have touched on pen and pen tip handling so that your pens will serve you as long as possible.

- Finally, we've looked at a starter list of the supplies that you will need to begin your pyrography project. You will not have a comprehensive list from the get-go, mainly because your circumstances are different from those of the next person. However, this chapter gives you the foundation to help you plan from a position of information.

In the next chapter, we will look at:

- Safety Measures in the Pyrography Workspace

CHAPTER THREE

SAFETY PRECAUTIONS IN THE PYROGRAPHY WORKSPACE

Pyrography is working with fire. Therefore, in the same way you would take regular precautions when working in the kitchen or with any other fire-based equipment, you must take precautions in pyrography. There are, however, a few extra precautions we will delve into that are important when working safely on your pyrography art and with the tools you're using. Let us dig right into it:

- *Select your work surface with extra care*

Before starting, take time to select your working area with care. It could be tempting to start in whatever area you find with a little bit of space. If that is the situation, make the area you select as safe as possible. You will, after all, be working with fire.

The working table should be stable. The electrical outlet should be at an angle that will not require you to jump over electrical cables. Consider extending your cabling so that it rests on the floor rather than let it dangle in the air.

Make sure the selected position for your pen is on a surface that is flat and stable. If you can secure the unit so that it is firmly in place and you only need to reach for the pen, that is even better. For peace of mind, it's highly recommended that you cover the tabletop so that you are not worrying about damaging it as you work.

- *Do not work on beds or on the couch*

Tempting as it is to start work immediately, it is a very bad idea to work on any surface covered in a material that can easily catch fire. This includes the bed, the couch, the carpet, a hayloft, and all such places. It is not that people are careless, but all sorts of distractions can lead to an accident leading to unimaginable damage to property and people.

To these we add, do not, for whatever reason, work on your lap. Clothes are prone to catch fire, and it wouldn't stop at your clothes - it would include your skin. You could end up with serious burns if an accident were to occur.

- *Work in a well-ventilated area*

As your wood comes into contact with the pen tip, there will be smoke. Make sure the wind takes the smoke away from your face. So as you plan your working space, take note of the direction of the table vis-à-vis the windows. Although the wind changes direction regularly, there is a general direction of the breeze in every room. Take that into account.

You may also consider installing a fan that will blow the smoke towards the windows and away from your face. The fan should only create a gentle breeze. It should not be too near you as that will dry the air you breathe too much. So, the fan should be at a distance creating a cool breeze, and blowing the smoke away and in the direction of the window. It should also not blow directly on your pen. It will force-cool the unit, which will make your system power-inefficient.

If you are going to sand your art before you start, wear your dust goggles. If you are going to work on a piece that is particularly smoky, wear your face mask.

- *Change your pen tips when the unit is off and cold*

Besides the higher risk of damaging your pen tips, trying to remove the pen tips when they are hot can lead to an accident. Always screw the tip on or off only after confirming that the heating unit is switched off and the pen has been turned off long enough for the tip to be cool. You may also add another level of safety by changing your pen tips using a pair of pliers.

If your pen tips are attached with screws, then do have a screwdriver ready for this step. Most wire-nib burners that come with replaceable tips will have tweezers specially made to enable you to safely remove the pen tip. Have a dish nearby where you can place the tip after removal. Such a dish should be heat-resistant.

- *Pyrography pen tips are hot; do not touch the pen tip*

Engrave it on your mind: never touch the tip of the wood burning pen if the unit is switched on! The material used in most pyrography pens will not "look" hot. The tendency is to touch the pen tip to test if it is hot. To test if the tip is hot, make it your habit to hover your hand over the tip. If it feels warm, you can be sure it is heating.

The other alternative is to touch the tip to a surface that you do not mind burning, but, obviously, never your skin. A good surface would be a piece of old wood that you are no longer using. It also can be a piece of wood you practice your burning technique on before you go to the main piece.

Although it may seem rather obvious advice that one should not touch the tip of the pen, many beginners do accidentally get this type of burn. Keep in mind that the pen tip is supposed to burn wood, bone, and such tough materials. It will not just scald your hand, it will scorch your skin to a sizzle. Not pleasant!

- *Keep Your Fingers Away from the Pen Tip*

31

On the face of it, wood burning may not be much different from pencil sketching, except you are sketching with fire. It is not uncommon to place your hands in a way as to hold down your medium with the fingers of your freehand and dangerously near the tip of the pen. To avoid a burn, hold the wood you are burning with the fingers of your freehand kept away from the pen tip. If you are moving the pen tip towards the fingers of your other hand, it may come into contact with your fingers accidentally.

The better style is to always hold your art with either tape or clamps to keep it steady. For good measure, keep in mind that holding your art with your hand may also ruin the wood if your hands are sweaty or oily.

- *Wear heat resistant gloves*

As an additional precaution, particularly if you find it difficult to shake the habit of holding your medium steady with your freehand, wear heat-insulated gloves. It is better to err on the side of caution, so beware that gloves can also be penetrated by the heat.

- *Keep your burner away from flammable substances*

Many who first start practicing the pyrography art do not have a dedicated space to do so. This means that you may find yourself making use of the least cluttered area in your garage or some other area that seems comfortable enough to get started. Clear out cans, compressed aerosols, inflammable liquids that could spill, and many materials with the "keep away from fire" labeling from around the working area. Check the space you choose to work in for loose cloths, regular pen holders, and other bits and pieces that may accidentally get caught on the edge of the pen. Be very careful with liquids. Burning flammable liquids can spread a fire in no time.

Another precaution is to avoid surfaces where inflammable fuels might be used or will be used. If you will work in a garage that could have inflammable chemical spills, make sure there is a shield between such a surface and your work.

- *Make it a habit to read the labels*

There are many chemical-based substances you will use with pyrography. If you choose to paint, you will use paints. Finishes are mostly chemical-based. Always make sure you read labels on the items you purchase to just be sure you know what is flammable and what isn't.

- *Clear your working space of accident hazards*

Ensure that nothing can accidentally come loose or in some way fall onto the area on which you are working. Clearing clutter will help keep your working area safer. Keep paper away from your working area as it can easily catch fire. This includes the pyrography designs that are not immediately in use. Also be careful about lightweight items that can be caught in a draught and land on your work.

- *Make a set storage area for your pen tips and other pen-sized accessories*

You could make this your first actual design project. Make a wooden unit where you can have an all-in-one place that gives easy access to all your pen tips. This could be moveable or immovable. The significant thing to keep in mind is the placement in relation to the hot pen tip or the ends of your pen. You can add all your pen-sized accessories to the wooden panel so that your tools are within easy reach at all times.

- *Dress with safety in mind*

Wear clothes or overalls that do not have hanging sleeves, sweeping sleeves, or sections that can get caught on edges. Loose-fitting clothes pose a risk. They could hook on to something and trigger a series of unforeseen accidents. If you have long hair, consider holding it in a bun or under a cap. You may also want to take off jewelry that could catch on things.

- *Plan the 'at-rest' position of your pyrography pen*

As in all art, you will develop habits around your work. Train yourself to always keep your pen tip facing away from the working table when it's not in use. If the unit came with a console, always return it to the console. The tendency could be to lay the pen aside to take a look at the progress of your work. It just leads to a bad habit that is also potentially dangerous.

- *Assume you will be gone longer a minute*

"I'll only be gone a minute" probably accounts for more accidents than we know. If you're going to leave your desk, switch off the electrical current. Even in situations when you think you will only be going to the next room or to the bathroom, switch it off. This habit further protects anyone else who may come into your working area in your absence. Equipment left unattended is a grave hazard. On leaving your desk for long stretches, switch off the pen and unplug it from the electrical outlet.

- *Select your wood type with both health and safety in mind*

In addition to the aesthetic look, consider the wood you will use with both health and safety in mind. Health in regards to the smoke that the wood will emit. Toxic smoke will affect you in the long term. Choose untreated, properly dry, well-seasoned, and non-toxic woods. We will cover wood types in the next chapter to help you identify other factors to keep in mind when selecting your wood.

If your art project requires another medium such as leather, bone, cork, etc, always choose untreated and unpainted pieces. If they are painted, then take the time to sand off the paint or the varnish and expose the untreated material.

- *Have dedicated storage positions for electrical equipment*

As with any craft that requires the use of high-temperature machinery, always take due care. If you will be gone for some time, store your equipment well away.

- *A quick word about children*

Children are curious, and a wood burning pen looks a lot like a pen and is deceptively innocent. If you have children, teach them to be careful around the equipment. If you have a toddler, keep them well away from your working area. The pen tips are shiny, small, and the perfect little thing for a child to swallow or push into their mouth - and that will end in an emergency room.

Remember, children are not usually dressed for the workshop. They are not reading this manual. They might not be aware of the seriousness of a hot piece of metal in contact with the wrong thing. Children can be forgetful. To be really safe, keep children away from your wood burning area. Children are the other reason it is a great habit to always leave your equipment unplugged.

Depending on the pet you have, if you have one, you might want to keep the same safety threshold as you would with children around your work area.

Chapter Summary

- We launched this chapter by emphasizing that pyrography is about working with fire. The pyrography pen is extremely hot and is designed to burn. It doesn't discriminate between burning wood or burning a human being. Internalize this as early as possible so you can get into pyrography with safety consciousness already in place.

- To fulfill that goal, we've discussed various aspects of safety. Included in these aspects are considerations within the working area and how to keep it safe. We have touched on a common accident with beginners and how to avoid it - touching the hot pen tip. In addition, we've discussed materials that could pose a safety hazard, other related equipment, and how a merger of all these different pieces can be structured to ensure safety in your workshop.

- Finally, we have mentioned safety measures that are important in relation to children and pets.

In the next chapter, we will look at:

- Choosing and Preparing Wood.

CHAPTER FOUR

CHOOSING AND PREPARING WOOD

There are numerous types of wood used in pyrography. There are some primary deciding factors, which we aim to cover in this chapter, but mainly you should consider the safety of the wood. You should also consider the color of the wood, especially at the beginning. The darker woods will require a lot more skill to bring out the effect of burning. Therefore go for the lighter woods. These will bring out the tones of your work in sharp contrast to the wood color.

Favor the lighter woods at the beginning.

Many argue that, depending on your machinery, you can utilize a large scope of different wood types as long as they are not toxic and do not give off harmful fumes when burning. While selecting the right wood for your project is a little more complicated than simply selecting hard or softwood, it is highly recommended that beginners practice on softwood. Balsa is very good in that respect.

Most pyrography artists prefer wood with the least possible grain, and balsa is ideal in this regard as well. It is easily accessible as it's used in many crafts and hobbies.

The main challenge in getting your hands on it is finding a suitable cut. All too often, it is only sold as blocks intended for modeling.

Basswood is another softwood option, although some find it so soft as to offer its own challenges. Similarly light in color and grain, Birch is perhaps the most easily accessible wood type that's ideal for beginners.

It is recommended that a novice or beginner look for wood with similar characteristics to these examples. But there are no rigid restrictions. To better understand why you might favor a particular set of characteristics, let us explore their qualities.

Choosing softwood or hardwood

Softwood is valued in the art of pyrography for the ease with which it can be worked. Not only is it simple to get an impression on, various effects such as shading and tinting are far easier to practice and perform on these types of wood. This is not to discount the value of hardwoods such as the highly sought after, hence more expensive, Maple wood. Hardwoods are reserved for use by experts due to the skill needed to wield them for pyrographic art.

These hardwoods do offer a crucial benefit. It is easier to correct mistakes on them. This is due to the high gauge-resistant nature that they tend to have. Hardwoods may also be lighter than softwoods, but this depends on the specific type.

Common wood types and their characteristics

Let us now delve deeper into the various wood types just to offer a frame of reference for some of the most commonly used types. There is a spectrum of variation in all the key factors, and the matter of tree sap also plays a significant role.

- Alder

The first is Alder, which is only infrequently used in pyrography. It has its good aspects - sap being pretty much a non-factor. It is only available in around four inch slats, and, although it burns easier than some softer woods, it is a tad dark.

- Balsa

The aforementioned Balsa wood is, as we have mentioned, very soft. This makes it one of the best substrates for pyrography practice. It is not well-suited to doing complete projects as it is far too easy to make small mistakes and it's impossible to rectify them.

- Basswood

The wood commonly called Basswood in the US, or Common Linden in the rest of the world, is perhaps one of the most popular woods used in pyrography. It is a softwood, and is easily machined. It is not as sensitive to the pyrography process as Balsa.

Basswood has an ideally light color, frequently with a yellow tone. It is inexpensive to acquire and quite readily

41

available in craft stores at appropriate sizes for working. Basswood has sparse grain and virtually no sap. It is not the easiest wood to amend mistakes on, however, due to how soft it is.

- Beech

Beech has some major failings as a pyrography medium, at least for most. It is a hardwood, and it is cheaper than maple, but it presents an unappealing challenge. The wood has a lot of knots and divots that produce sap under heating. The grain on Beech also has a tendency to darken, which, if used intentionally in a design, may provide a certain aesthetic, but is commonly not a sought-after quality. The wood also has a curiously dotted surface.

- Cherry

Cherry is a hardwood that is very popular among most woodworking crafts and is easy to source. It is less expensive than maple, but does come with a number of caveats, not only due to it being of the hardwood variety. Cherry is fantastic for any items that may be handled frequently due to its resilience, but the wood tends to be quite dark with a non-uniform color disbursement. This, in addition to how easily it darkens under various treatments, means that any pyrography artwork may not stand out prominently.

- Hickory

Hickory wood is another feasible but unpopular option. Used widely in carpentry, the wood has excessive color variations. These variations extend to the machining 'feel' since different areas may respond to heat slightly differently.

It is a wood that almost serves as a 'what not to use' example when looking for pyrography substrates. It is not the most inexpensive on the list, and in conjunction with the aforementioned variations in color, the grain is also very pronounced. It's a great challenge for advanced practice should you have some discarded scraps lying around, but it is not easy to recommend.

- Maple

Coming back to Maple, it is what you might consider a 'premium' pyrography substrate. It is a hardwood favored by the skilled pyrography artist. It is also light and can sport minimal grain. Note that 'can' is a word that should be underlined as one also finds variants that have more grain than others.

It is generally available for purchase in hardware stores, and is an excellent medium for furniture and other items that benefit from its resilience. Its gouge resistance makes editing mistakes much easier than in softwoods. It is definitely a medium for professionals.

- Mahogany

Mahogany is an easy wood to burn on. This does not mean you are necessarily going to expect the best results. It is astonishingly expensive and has a grain that darkens distinctly under heat. For specifically intended designs this may be great, but, otherwise, it is not recommended.

- Oak

Oak is another wood that is very popular in carpentry and it enjoys a historic reputation for quality. This reputation does not extend to the world of pyrography, unfortunately. A streaked finish with an impossible to circumnavigate grain makes this wood unpopular with pyrography artists.

- Pacific Albus

Pacific Albus is a hybrid variant. This would be the ideal softwood for practice were it not rather rare in the U.S. Sharing many of the qualities associated with Balsa wood, it's also very inexpensive. It does suffer from its heat sensitivity; when burning dark features, the tip of your pen may easily sink into the wood.

- Pine

Pine is one of the easiest substrates to come across. But, for the purposes of pyrography, it suffers from its high levels of sap. That means that under intense heat, you are bound to find bubbling-up sap and be left with sticky spots across your artwork.

- Plywood

Plywood, while technically still a plausible option, is not advisable, particularly for beginners. The very thin upper layer can easily be pierced, exposing toxic fumes under high heat. Furthermore, it does tend to have a bit of a texture and artwork tends to fade.

- Poplar

Poplar is a very good alternative to Maple. It is a durable hardwood frequently used in carpentry. It is perfect for items that need extra resilience, and it shares many of the other qualities commonly associated with Maple. It's a popular wood for our purposes.

Most importantly, Poplar is substantially less costly. It does have a few shortcomings. Given that it is commonly only found in smaller slats, you may have to combine slats to form a suitably sized medium. It may sometimes feature areas of varying color. These areas, forming intermittent streaks, release sap under the heat of burning, which isn't ideal.

- Redwood

Redwood brings us back to the unpopular side of the spectrum, with the wood being understandably difficult to work due to various red features patterned throughout the wood surface. These areas release sap under high temperatures.

- Walnut

Continuing our list of unpopular options, Walnut is a characteristically dark wood that may be rather easy to burn, but does not endear itself to pyrography artists due to how dark it is. Artwork often fades to an almost indiscernible degree.

It may take some experimentation to find the type of wood that suits you, but the above should serve as a helpful guideline. Once you have decided on the type of wood you prefer to use, it is time to get it prepared for pyrography.

Where to source wood for pyrography

Before you get into the actual pyrographic burning, pick up or create some practice boards. These are cut pieces of wood that you can burn as practice runs for your techniques.

There isn't one wood source that works for everyone. Whilst you can purchase prepared slats of wood referred to as studio panels, it may not always be easy to source a specific type of wood. You may also be on a budget and ideal pieces will be pricier.

Many artists prefer to prepare their own wood. It adds to the joy of the art and in the finished product. Eventually, you will find what's best for you. However, there are a few pointers that will lead you in the right direction, especially when you are starting out.

• Remember that the quality of wood matters

It is worth repeating that for pyrography, you want to avoid treated wood. That will include painted wood, wood items with a veneer, varnish, oil, wax, or any other type of finish. The chemical in these finishes will most likely be toxic when subjected to the wood burning heat. The smoke will irritate your lungs and your eyes.

• Household items for practice

That said, you can sand off the treated coating on household items to get to the untreated wood beneath. You can get very creative on the household items you decide to burn. These will range from wooden spoons to antique pieces of furniture, and anything in between.

The wood in these items will not necessarily be what you want, but it will still give you great practice on what your pen can do.

You might want to expand your reach and visit with friends and neighbors or other pyrography enthusiasts and see who will have a piece you can work with. They can also give you advice. You may just come by a great piece that someone does not need and that you can buy for a few bucks.

• Local Timber Yards

Speak to the timber yards and widen your reach to the lumber yards in your local area. Those will not only know the wood by name and by look, but will give you useful tips on the way wood behaves in certain conditions. In other words, you will be speaking with wood experts.

Other local suppliers that will be of great help include furniture makers and carpenters. They will also help you find wood at more affordable prices in the local vicinity. If there are festivals that focus on wood or wood items, don't miss those. You will find some great tips and possibly a lovely piece of wood.

- Craft stores both offline and online

As soon as you start your pyrography journey, you will start to see stores that you possibly hadn't noticed before. Some of these might be craft stores. Pop in, and you will almost certainly find lovely pieces. Most of the pieces available will depend on where you are and the main buyers the craft shop supplies.

The sure source for wood will be online. That's where you can get the size you want and the exact wood you are looking for. Amazon stands head and shoulders above most online stores. Other online stores include AliExpress and Etsy, just to name a few. Based on where you are, a quick search will give you the other options in your area.

Chapter Summary

- We launched the chapter on woods used in pyrography by mentioning that the beginner needs to keep their focus on the lighter-colored woods. The darker woods will require a lot more skill to bring out the results of the burning. The effort may discourage the beginner.

- The chapter further outlines a list of common woods, mentions their characteristics, and their suitability for wood burning. We've looked at places to source your woods. The main aim of this section is to ensure that you know how to find your desired types of wood in your vicinity.

- Also mentioned are other types of wood pieces you can use for practice, including those around you. As you get into the chapter, you will find that pyrography is an art just waiting for you to start. The opportunities and possible materials you can use are all around you.

In the next chapter, we will discuss:

- How to prepare your wood for pyrography.

CHAPTER FIVE

HOW TO PREPARE YOUR WOOD

You have an idea about what you might need to start your pyrography project. You have your first piece of wood. Now you want to get a feel of what you need to do to actually start creating the art. In this chapter, we will discuss how to prepare your workspace, how to ready your wood, and how to transfer your design to your wood.

To get the process right, you will need the following items:

- A clear working table or surface. No clutter, no bits and pieces that might fall off the table as you work.

- A cover sheet for your working surface. This could be a towel, a foam liner, or any other material that will not slip as you work. The purpose of this sheet is to gather the shards that will come off your piece of wood.

- Sandpaper and it's accessory if you have one, such as a sandpaper holder.

- You will also need your design and your design transfer materials.

- Your piece of wood, of course.

Let us get right into it:

Before you start, make sure you are dressed for the task at hand. Changing into your work clothes is best at this point. Keep your goggles, your face mask, and your earplugs within easy reach. You will only need earplugs with the electric sander. The manual sanding process will not need earplugs.

Now you need to prepare your working table or surface. Start by laying your cover sheet on the working surface. The sheet could be an old towel or a foam sheet. The sheet should cover as much as possible, but you definitely want it to cover the space immediately below your hands and wood.

Sanding will produce dust and wood fragments that will spread on your working surface. The larger fragments can scratch the bottom of your piece and damage your artwork. A cover sheet protects your surface from this waste and your wood by cushioning the fragments. It also makes cleaning up after you have completed the sanding process much easier and faster. You just gather the waste in the middle of the sheet and throw it away. The other advantage of having a cover sheet is that it gives you a better grip on the wood. If you are working with an electric sander, the wiggle on the wood can slow down your progress significantly.

With that in place, prepare your sandpaper. If you have a sander, either hand-held or electric, put your sandpaper in place.

QUICK TIP: if you need to work on more than one piece of wood, allocate a chunk of time to sand all of them at once. Think process! The dressing, preparing your work table, and getting all the equipment takes time. So crunch the time into one segment. Call it a "sandpaper morning" or something.

Now we come to sanding the wood. The main purpose of this is to get a smooth finish on it. You want to get the grooves out and leave a consistent, groove-free, buttery kind of feel to the side of the wood you will draw on. It is tempting to skip this stage because it feels like quite a drag. However, you will appreciate it once you start working. It will save you loads of time and frustration when you start burning if your wood is smooth. You are less likely to get an over-burnt spot because the wood burning pen got caught in a groove if you have grooves.

If you have the skill, go ahead and get right into using the electric sander. If you hardly know how to hold one, you may want to work with a manual sandpaper holder for now.

A word about the electric sander; it will vibrate a lot making your hand uncomfortably tingly. To absorb most of the vibration, use gloves. If you try it once and the tingle is too much, you can check out a pair of anti-itch gloves that are made specifically for people who work with electrical equipment with a buzz. It will also help if your piece is steady, rather than moving about. The right grit sandpaper also enhances your sanding process a whole lot.

Always sand in the same direction as the grain of the wood, never against the grain. Sand in a continuing motion from one end of your piece to the other. You will choose your sandpaper grit by the level of sanding you need to do.

If your wood has a lot of grooves and rough patches, start with medium grit at between 80 to 120. If you need a lower grit paper, you may go to the lower grit at 40 to 60 grit. Work your way upwards to a smooth finish with extra fine sandpaper at 280 to 320 grit. If you go above that, your wood will be too "polished" to serve your purpose.

As your piece of wood becomes smoother, dab at the surface with a wet sponge to remove the fine dust so that it does not get back on the surface creating tiny grooves. This must not be a lot of water. It is just dabbing at the surface. When you are done with sanding your wood, set it aside to dry. Once dry, gently pass the super fine sandpaper once more on the surface. You should have a very smooth substrate on which to work. You wet the wood to raise the grain so that you get a smooth finish.

QUICK TIP: Sometimes you'll have dents or some areas where the wood is raised. It's as though it has a wrinkle. That wrinkle does not need to be sanded. Rather, take your transfer tip, a flat headed tip, or the shading point. The shading point looks almost like the nib of a fountain pen.

Spray a little water on the segment, or use a damp sponge with very little water. It will raise the dents on the wood. Then, as you pass your pen point over the segment, set to low heat. It should not be hot enough to burn, but not hot enough to dry. This tactic works much like removing creases off a garment.

You may want to consider drawing with pencils. Since this is not a fine art book, we will keep this section short. To briefly mention the difference in pencils, there are two main types - graphite and charcoal. Generally, the pencils you will commonly encounter are graphite pencils. Charcoal pencils are less common, but are great for putting a sketch together.

For setting up your pyrography art on your wood, what you are looking for is a pencil that will not have unnecessarily dark lines, but be clear enough for you to be able to burn inside the image outline. We are going to detail three main methods of image transfer that will work for the beginner.

There are many ways of transferring your image to the wood before burning. This guide will give you a starting point. We will start with the best method and then go on and discuss alternative methods. For most of your work, you may eventually settle on just one approach. It is always good to know several as you progress. The method will be influenced by the shape of your media and the kind of image you want to transfer.

- *Using graphite or transfer paper*

Graphite paper, also known as transfer paper in the art community, is one of the best supplies to have in your pyrography purchases. If you are a bit older, it works in the same way as carbon paper. If you were born after the photocopier became a thing, then carbon paper was how copying was done in ancient days!

Basically, you place the medium beneath, with the side you want to transfer your image on facing up. Then you tape or clamp your design, cut to size, on your piece of wood. Many pyrography artists swear by a laser-printed image. Usually a laser-printed artwork is clearer and transfers better than ink jet-printed images.

You then place transfer paper beneath the art and draw the outline in freehand. What you need to be aware of is how your hand is rubbing on the paper. This can leave smudges on your wood. A smudge will give you an extra cleaning task.

So what happens if you do not have graphite paper? The alternative is to use carbon paper.

- *Transfer with carbon paper*

The main difference between carbon and graphite paper is that the former is more sensitive to pressure and needs more care to work with. Also, carbon paper is waxed on the side in direct contact with your art. This may leave marks on your piece of wood.

You use the same technique as with the graphite paper. Place the printed artwork on the wood and use tape or clamps to hold it in place. Then take your carbon paper and gently slip it beneath the paper and on top of the wood with the inked side facing the wood.

Draw your outline on the wood, being careful not to rub your hand on the carbon paper as this will definitely leave blotches of clack on your wood.

- *Shading with a pencil*

What happens if you do not have the carbon or graphite paper available? This next method will save the day. It is a bit cumbersome and does not give you outstanding results, but it will work.

For this method of transfer, shade the back of your paper to get a kind of carbon look on the back. A charcoal pencil will give you better results for this type of shading.

Then draw your art in freehand on the front side, while holding the paper on the wood.

Hold the paper in place with tape or clamps. The other alternative is to have the drawing already done. You can use a printed image. Shade the back of the paper along the outline of the image. Then redraw the art along the outlines and on your piece of wood.

This method does not give a very well-defined image. It will work if you do not have either of the other two previous options available.

QUICK TIP: your image should be a proper fit on your piece of wood.

You may explore other methods of image transfer, but these ones will serve you as a starting point. Once you have your image done, you are now ready to start shading in your art. In the next chapter, we will discuss how to choose your design and what pen tip will work for different types of shading.

Chapter Summary

- In this chapter, we started by highlighting the most basic items that you will need to launch a pyrography project. You should have gained a very clear idea of where to start when you choose to take on pyrography.

- Once again, we have mentioned safety because it really is important. We have then discussed areas of preparation that will make it easier to launch your project. The chapter includes practical skills such as using a sandpaper, an electric sander, and has introduced the topic of various image-transfer methods.

- Finally, we have discussed scenarios where you might not have everything mentioned. If that is the case, we have highlighted alternatives that are more readily available. This is in recognition of the likelihood that not everyone will have a craft shop nearby. The goal of this chapter is to give the reader a view that demystifies pyrography and makes it an art form they can begin with ease.

In the next chapter, we will look at:

- How to choose a pen tip and starter pyrography techniques.

CHAPTER SIX

CHOOSING A PEN TIP AND PYROGRAPHY TECHNIQUES

As mentioned in the first description of pens and pen tips, there are two main types. In this section, we'll add a bit more detail. This deeper knowledge will enable you to choose the best pen and pen tips for your art. Let us get right into it.

First, remember that your pen handling technique is the most important part of wood burning. How well you can maneuver your pen over your work is what will make a difference between average skill and pro-skill. Using the wrong pen tip will result in a number of difficulties as you work.

The primary problem will be art that appears smudged. Clean lines, fine shading, and fine detail are what gives that "Oh, my!" quality to what you create. So pay keen attention to your pens. How you and your tools work together is crucial.

Understanding pyrography pens

Pyrography pens come in three categories: writers, shaders, and skews. This is true of both solid-point burners as well as wire-tip burners. Some manufactures add more pen tips in a category usually tagged as "other" in most pyrography circuits. These will mostly be decorative tips that will help to enhance your designs, but are not entirely necessary.

Many pyrography artists hardly ever go to the extent of using these additional tips, as, with practice, you can achieve the same result with skillful use of pens in the three main categories. Much of your art skill will be covered with the use of a pen tip or two, and at most, three - that is one in each of the three categories.

- Writers

The writer pen tip is the most basic type and the one that you will use for the bulk of your work. The writer looks a lot like the ordinary pen. It will taper towards the top and give you a focused burning tip. In the solid-point burner, it will be cylindrical with a tapering tip.

In the wire tip burner, they will have the same general design but in a sort of silhouette appearance. The tapering will be achieved by the thin wire at the top of the pen. It will be bent wire with a small ball at the corner point giving a nib-like appearance. It is important to appreciate the difference between the writers and the shaders as some may have an almost similar appearance. The best way to easily identify the pen tip is to look at it and practically assess its possible use. The description of the other two major categories will always guide you in identifying the pen tips to use.

In some kits, the writers in the kit will have a ball with a rounded edge at the tip. The ball and rounded edge on the cutting point enables you to achieve an easy flow over the wood grain. It does not cut into the wood and gives you more control so that you can move your pen tip in the direction you want to take your pen.

With the writer, you can achieve a gliding motion, a sweeping motion, and a dotting motion. It is the pen tip that will enable you to make the most basic design elements, namely the line, the dot, the circle, and the wavy lines. To get a sharper line, you can turn the pen in your hand so that the sharpest point is in contact with your medium.

- Shaders

The shader pen tip.

Shader pen tips will have a flattish appearance and a 45-degree angle at the top. In the solid-point burner, they will look a bit like a miniature shovel. In the wire-point burner, they will deviate at a 45-degree angle at the tip and will have the two wires running parallel to each other giving the shovel-like look on top.

The purpose of shaders is, as the name suggests, to shade. By holding the pen tip at a 45-degree angle to the medium, you can sweep over the wood and achieve a burn according to the effect you want to achieve. We will get into that in more detail when we discuss tones.

- **S**kews

Where the writer has a sharp point, the skew tip tapers like a knife edge. It is also called a universal edge in some circuits. Tips that have the knife edge have multiple uses. It is a great pen to create a really thin line. It also has a burn edge that, when held at an angle to the medium, will work well as a shader.

The skew tip is ideal for the longer straight lines you would need to burn to illustrate hair or a grass patch. You can get a deep and yet thin, dark burn. If you are going to use this type of pen tip for shading, you might have to use the crosshatching shading method. We will get into how to use these design techniques in the chapter on design.

These pen tip categories are not universal. Different manufactures will label the pen tips with a different name. You need to keep in mind the use of the pen more than the name.

You will easily identify each pen's use with its overall design. Remember, the really pointy type is good for drawing just as you would with a regular pen. The flat for shading and the pen tip that has both can be used for more than one purpose.

The pen tips in one range

Some burning kits will have only a few pen tips. The most basic pen tips in such a kit will include the following tips. A writer with a ballpoint tip, which is a visibly rounded tip at the end. This is the most natural for most people when they want to achieve a similar technique to ordinary writing. Wood burning lettering is beautifully achieved with this pen tip.

The kit might also have a piece out of the skew tip range. It will have a tapering top and lean at an angle at the top. This pen has a tiny sharp point that will be great for burning the long lines you would require on larger pieces of art.

Other tips might be the pointed edge tip that looks like the fine art pencil point. This is a good pyrography tip to maneuver the burn into tighter spots. Developing a portrait might require this tip. Another common tip that will be added is the circular point. The circular tip will have a flattish ball at the top. It is ideal for developing wider lines that do not cut into the wood. You will get a smooth move across the wood with this tip. The universal tip is a standard addition to all wood burning tip units. It is a versatile tool. It is also the one that you will find on the single burner unit.

There are a variety of names given to pyrography pen tips. Most are determined by the use and the manufacturer. The shape of the pen tip will also influence the name it is given. To give a wider view of some more of the names you might encounter, here are some.

1. Universal Point

2. Mini Universal Point

3. Calligraphy Point

4. Flow Point

5. Mini Flow Point

6. Cone Point

7. Shading Point

8. Tapered Point

9. Transfer Point

10. Hot Knife Point

11. Hot Stamp Points

Wood burning techniques

Now that you know what pen tip to use, we will discuss various ways to turn your medium from a flat one color piece of wood to pure art. In this section, we will discuss how to achieve various tonal variations. We will also discuss the merger between art techniques and how to apply them to pyrography.

We will start with your practice run. To get on with this, have your prepared piece of wood ready, sit at your workplace, and make sure you take all the safety precautions. Now go ahead and switch your pyrography pen on. Making sure you have the tip attached securely if you are using a removable tip.

Learning your pen-in-hand

Practice what your pen feels like in your hand. You do this by creating the basic art shapes. The basic art shapes are lines, circles, wavy lines, dots, squares, and triangles. You can practice drawing each one, increasing the pressure on your pen tip with each new stroke. This will give you an idea of how your pen will behave with pressure.

Be sure not to exert too much pressure as to bend or break the pen tip. As it grows hotter, it is easier to bend it. Keep a feel of what is happening with your tip. Your tools should follow your lead. Always remember you are in charge of the tool, the tool is not in charge of you.

Change the drawing you have by changing the use of the pen tip. There are important uses that you can vary to see the results you get.

1. The direction in which the tip is sitting on the wood. This includes the angle at which you hold the tip in relation to the wood. As a general skill, move the wood around and not the pen.

2. How much pressure you place on the wood.

3. The speed at which you move it across the board.

If you have different pen tips, you may experiment with the same different shapes with different pens. You can record your lessons as you go. The notes will come in handy later, at least until you have developed your own style.

Keep a record of your practice results.

•   The pen temperature selection

The temperature of your wood burning pen will give you different shading tones. It's highly recommended that you use a pen with an adjustable temperature unit. It gives you more control over the shade you want to achieve, from the lightest to the darkest.

When you start shading, vary this setting, raising the temperature on your pen gradually. You can jump in a unit or in sets of five units on the temperature scale. You will evaluate if one unit is too little or five is too much.

Types of shading

As we will see in the next section, there are two fundamental tonal values from really light and nearly invisible to really dark and black. To achieve various tonal values, you can use different basic shading techniques. We will discuss them in greater detail in the next chapter, but here they are in brief.

- Circular shading

Using circular shading is like the pencil equivalent of circular shading, but this time using a shading pen tip. With your shading tip set to lowest heat, start moving your pen tip in a small circular motion on the test-wood. Keep turning the heat up and see the new tone you get, maintaining the same shading speed and using the same shading style.

Shading in a circular pattern.

- Pulling motion

Using a shader, pull it from one end of a designated section and across the wood. The idea is to try and maintain the same tonal value across the area. In the second trial, move the tone from the lowest to the darkest tonal value you can achieve with the same temperature.

Shading using the pulling motion.

- The dot pattern or stripling

Use the round pen tip shade in a sample circle or square with dots. Once again, you want to maintain the same shade in a box and also gradually increase the tonal-value in the same box. You can shade in from the lowest tonal shade to the darkest within the same box.

The Tonal Values Panel

The next practice run will be to create a "tonal values panel." Tonal values panel is a term derived from the art concept of "tone." In other words, the "relative lightness or darkness of a colour" developed on the practice piece of wood. The concept of a tonal values panel is a brilliant idea and has been adopted from Lora Irish.

The idea behind creating a "tonal value panel" is to have your own catalog of the tone you achieve with a different pen tip, technique, and temperature.

We will use the same training method as one does with traditional shading. Start by drawing three boxes. Start with the lowest heat and shade in the first box. Then move to the highest temperature. Shade in using that temperature. Finally, use the middle level temperature and shade in using that too.

Now that you have the middle, the lowest, and the highest, you can create your own tonal value panel. Establish the points you will adjust the temperature to shade in an increasing tone in seven boxes moving from the lightest to the darkest.

Practice your tonal values from the lightest to the darkest.

Choose a shading technique that you will use for shading in all the five boxes. We will discuss more shading techniques in the next chapter. Using your burner start at the lowest heat, shade in. Then increase the heat, and shade in. Keep that momentum going until you have a shade that goes from hardly noticeable to black.

On the column beside each box, write the temperature that you used to get that tone. Use the tonal value in the illustration to match your work to a scale. Don't fret if you find that you struggle to match the overall tone in the block, or if you accidentally gouge the wood.

This exercise simultaneously helps you learn about the different heat levels of your wire-nib pen, and the limitations of the medium you're using. We will repeat this same exercise numerous times to get a good feel for it.

Practice different shading techniques with the three-box panel. Once you have managed the right-hand side block, we will do the left-hand side block. This time we will focus on doing a shade only slightly darker than the natural shade of your medium. In other words, we will do the lightest possible shading you can manage.

Once again, don't worry should you struggle or make any mistakes. This block helps you get a feel for the subtlety and precision offered by the lower heat settings of your pen.

Once you have finished with the block to the left it is time for the center block. Using what you have learned from the left-and the right-hand blocks, it is time for you to do your best to create a perfect medium shade.

Do not worry too much about a 'perfect' result; this is simply your best initial attempt. Doing this helps you practice a combination of the skills learned and teaches you to find the balance between heat and pressure.

Once you feel that you have made progress with your technique, congratulations, you have learned to improve your skill with tone work, all while making your own shading exercise.

- Blur the tonal blocks

It is time to use these blocks to learn how to do shade work. The practice is to blend the border between the three blocks so that the distinguishing lines separating the blocks, their tonal difference, become 'blurred.'

To do this, you start in the darker of the two blocks you are blending and progressively lighten the area in indiscreet stages into the lighter block. While some people prefer to work into the lighter area in small areas, repeating the process over and over again, it is recommended that you shade 'vertically,' moving in stages to the left as you complete a new phase of shading into the lighter block.

It is also easiest to start in the darkest block and shade into the middle tone. After finishing with that, repeat the process for the mid-to-lighter tone. You will do this for all the tonal blocks you have created.

As mentioned, shading is not an easy skill to master. It takes many hours over many days, if not weeks, for sketch artists to master the techniques. Pyrography is arguably a more challenging art form for applying this skill.

Once you have mastered the three blocks, move to improving your skill in five blocks. The utmost right-hand-sided block will be burnt the same tone as its counterpart on your three-block training set. If you are still struggling to replicate the precise tone, you may need to continue your practice with the three-block set.

In the same way, the utmost left-hand block will be the same light tone as its counterpart on the three-block set. The center, or third block on your five-block set, must match up to your middle block on the three-block set.

It may be clear what your next practice will be. Make sure your two new tones are one mid-point in darkness between your right-hand side block and center block, the other a mid-point between your middle and left-most block.

Once you have completed your tonal palette, it is not yet time to move on to shading. Repeat the process a few times, at least until replicating the tones feels natural. After this, you will repeat the shading technique used on the three-block set, blending the tones across the tonal border between each block.

Your next and final shading practice will be a repeat of the same process, this time with eight blocks. The logical progression would be seven. However, the additional block serves a purpose. As with your five-block set, you will add a shade between each of the shades from your five-block set.

The eighth block will be where you practice shading to the natural tone of the substrate. In other words, shading to blank. You will repeat this process until you are comfortable with all the shades and tones you have created.

You may decide to continue this process of adding intermittent shades, and it is highly recommended you do. Only once you have mastered a true gradient (when the shades between blocks are so slightly different that looking at the entire sequence looks like a shaded monochrome gradient without you having done any deliberate shading) will you really have mastered shading and tonal work.

Chapter Summary

- At the beginning of this book, we mentioned pen and pen tips. In the chapter above, we delve deeper into the topic of pens and pen tips. There is tons of information out there and it is easy to get both confused and overwhelmed. So we have set out to give the reader a clear picture of the wide-ranging topic of pens and pen tips and how to navigate through the information available.

- The chapter reduces what is an otherwise complicated topic into a bite-size chunk. This narrows down the information to absolute basics, defines the common categorizations used by brand developers, and gives details on how to lay the foundation for all pyrography pens and pen tips. The chapter also takes the reader through wood burning techniques.

- The information has endeavored to present the relationship between the way artists understand their pen and the results they get from their tools. We have delved into shading as one of the primary aspects of wood burning. Finally, we have linked up with the universal standard on tones with practical skills to help the reader practice their shading skills.

In the next chapter, we will discuss:

- Shading techniques for more variety.

CHAPTER SEVEN

SHADING TECHNIQUES

In this chapter, we will discuss a few more shading styles. We will then give a detailed look at cross-hatching and stippling, as these are two very common techniques. A number of pyrography artists find these shading styles easy to adopt. Later in the chapter, we will discuss designs and move on to sources of designs and inspiration for your art.

The Zentangle

The first shading method we will discuss is the Zentangle. This is a focused way of filling in art with the use of seemingly random shapes. The artists can fill in the selected design with a combination of curves, circles, dots, lines, squares, all in a seemingly random way, but one that brings out the art.

The 'zentangle' combines various basic shapes to fill into the larger design outline.

The Zentangle method of shading has gained prominence in modern times. Many users and enthusiasts argue that it is a method quite removed from the common doodle. In doodling, they say, the artist is generally bored and not particularly intentional in the work they are creating.

The primary value of the zentangle method is to choose the pen strokes you will burn with deliberate intention. The patterns are called tangles. It is like assembling different pieces in a mosaic, but this time with your pyrography burner.

Contour lines

Another fun shading method is the contour lines method. Contour lines follow the outline of the object and, in increasing density, shape the object and give it depth. You can work with contour lines on many objects with a definite outline or figure drawings. In this case, you draw the lines with the pyrography pen. The contour lines are the shading on the object rather than adding a shade to it for depth.

As an art technique, the lines follow the outline of the object, such as trees or landscapes, and along the same general line as the eye would naturally use. The increasing number of lines per level creates form, defines the edges, or sharpens shadow in the object in focus.

Parallel line hatching

Another variation of the use of lines is parallel line hatching. This varies from cross-hatching in that the lines run alongside each other in parallel formation. This is a painstaking method to use to shade. However, if you want to create something that could be excellent, try your hand at parallel hatching with your pyrography pen.

Cross-hatching in pyrography work

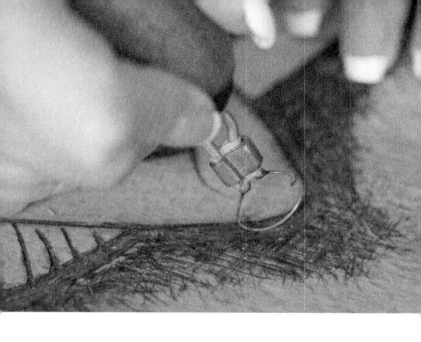

Shading in cross-hatching.

The next technique related to shading that you may find useful is hatching and cross-hatching. These techniques are incredibly common in pyrography. Whereas other disciplines may not focus on them, or even require their use at all, they are a set of sensible methods for a pyrography enthusiast to learn.

Hatching is a form of shading utilizing fine line work to create the impression of shading. You may have seen hatching on money and in vintage illustrations. Normal hatching differs from cross-hatching in that the lines to dot intersect, running in parallel to each other.

To start off with, we need to practice the most basic principle of hatching; maintaining an equal spacing between your lines as you follow form. We will also

81

attempt to understand this emphasis on form as we practice.

Start by burning a straight line ending in a curve or wave. The line shape does not matter as much as simply having a straight reference as well as a reference that curves on the same line segment.

It is important for this initial line to be as light as possible. You will repeat the line roughly a millimeter below the first line, then above, so make sure your initial line is vertically centered to your medium.

You must ensure that each line is as close as possible to the same weight (thickness), keeping them all light. Next, you will gently go halfway over the straight section and halfway over the curves section, allowing these sections to burn just slightly darker than the initial lines.

Next, you will do the same with the now darkened section of each line, halving that area by darkening the line slightly more. Repeat this process until the final line area is too small to make any significant additions.

You have now successfully practiced basic hatching. As you can see on your practice art, the darkening effect over lines with minimal variation in weight creates a shading effect. Once you have mastered the technique, you can start giving consideration to using it to affect form.

Hatching is a particularly good method for creating form and dimension. The line work also acts as guiding lines for the eye when viewing an artwork, so you can essentially 'sculpt' an object by taking into account the line direction and shade.

Cross-hatching is then the combination of multiple (most commonly two) perpendicular sets of parallel-hatching. Whereas hatching is, in principle, simple to practice, cross-hatching requires an understanding of the 'direction' of form. While hatching can be used to define specific areas and distinguish aspects of surfaces, cross-hatching allows you to imply volume.

This means that when you have a particular volumetric density, you can use contrast and cross-hatching to portray the difference rather effectively. As you master hatching and cross-hatching, you'll want to aim for fine and subtle implementations that allow you to incorporate the techniques alongside conventional shading.

The skills involved in these two primary forms of hatching will allow you to incorporate the more unique forms often used by visual and graphic artists. There is, for example, a hatching technique commonly referred to as weave hatching, in which two sets of perpendicular hatching follow the form of the object depicted in their respective direction, creating a woven 'scrappy' effect.

Tick Hatching

Another interesting technique predominantly used by graphic artists is referred to as 'tick-hatching,' a laborious practice where fine, dense areas of 'tick lines' are used to depict shadow and shaded areas. You can achieve a similar effect with the pyrography pen by nicking at the wood with the square corner of your pen tip. Look through the pen tips you have and find one that has a square edge if placed at 45 degrees to the wood.

Stippling

Stippling shading uses dots to create a sense of darker and lighter areas.

Moving on from hatching, a technique that plays an important role in shading, particularly in pyrography, is a

84

method called stippling. It is one of the most impressive forms of shading, with its roots preceding its association with the early days of printing.

Stippling is the process of creating shading and texture through fine dots. The important thing to be aware of is that the shading is not produced by the darkness of any individual dots. All the dots used to shade in this way are meant to be the same tone, with the visual illusion created by the density of the dots.

The connection commonly made with the early days of printing is that the 'resolution' involved meant that prints had clearly visible dots making up the desired image as a whole. You might still see this in newspaper printing to this day.

The way in which dots are added, being denser to represent darker areas and less so for lighter areas, with areas devoid of dots creating the overexposure effect, does have consequences. It means there will be darkening of individual dots as one repeats the process of adding more dots in a 'darker' area.

The way that this is used in pyrography, and artworks in general, dictates that one should not try to accomplish conformity in the distribution of your stippling, but increase the density as needed.

One of the key things to keep in mind is that all the shading techniques we have discussed can be used together. Eventually, you will begin to truly breathe life into your pyrography artworks.

Chapter Summary

- In this chapter, we have taken the reader through the more advanced shading styles. Shading skills are what move the pyrography art a notch higher and turn the use of fire into sheer art.

- We've used shading techniques as a way of discussing how to use the pyrography pen. We've looked at how you can use basic art forms, namely, lines, circles, and other shapes, to add tone and depth to the work. The shading techniques discussed include contour lines, parallel line hatching, cross-hatching, and stippling, among others.

- In this chapter, the reader will have discovered there is so much they can do with the pyrography pen.

In the next chapter, we will discuss:

- Design and pattern ideas for pyrography.

CHAPTER EIGHT

DESIGN AND PATTERN IDEAS

In an earlier chapter, we discussed how to start your work. We referred to the transfer of a design several times. In this chapter, we wish to discuss uses of patterns, various types of designs, and where to find ideas. We will focus on patterns and designs that can enhance your pyrography art. When selecting images to use as designs, it is a great idea to take a deliberate approach, choosing designs that best allow for learning how to apply contour, tone, and texture. This way, you can practice combining your shading techniques to full effect.

Now that you have started burning on your practice piece of wood, keep in mind that the greatest art teacher is practice and more practice. Go over your techniques as well as experiment on different aspects of developing the art. This manual is an introduction. Practice will give you the confidence to use your skills in many more ways.

The points to remember in practical wood burning

Practice each technique methodically prior to dedicating time and effort to a design that requires a combination of many basic forms. Go over your line work, your circles, your dots, but, most significantly, work on your shading technique. As your line work skill improves, your challenge will be to continuously do finer detailed line work, steadily improving on your skills.

Once you are quite comfortable with line work and have done a number of complete projects to hone your ability, you may want to move on to more complex shading. This is a far more challenging skill to master. It depends on practical ability and also a talent that's similar to that of sketching.

As you get more comfortable with the feel of the wood burning pen in your hand and working on wood, take the next step and start finding a suitable design. Choosing a beautiful and complex design with various elements may be tempting, it is recommended that you choose strategically according to the skillsets required to do a design.

In this section, we will help you identify what to look for in identifying a design. Some items may not look like it, but from an art perspective, they're a combination of different lines.

Creating patterns with your pen tips

Most patterns are a repetition of the same initial and basic form repeated over many times. The beauty of a pattern in pyrography is the practice you get. If you choose to create a pattern with circles, then you will not repeat the circle in a monotonous rhythm, but, rather, you are intentional. There is a deliberate outcome you're aiming for at the end of the repetition.

The easiest design to start with to shade in with patterns is a string of letters. We will get into the design techniques later, but words are the easiest place to start. There are so many things you can beautify with a word, a letter, a pattern, or just a spattering for lines and dots.

Patterns are an excellent way to practice your shading abilities. You have no pressure on the expanse of the piece of wood, yet at the end of it, the art you have created will still be beautiful to look at. The dotted pattern is an excellent way to practice using dots as your shading technique.

Patterns can also be sourced from craft shops. Use these to transfer the pattern to your medium and have fun with what you're doing.

Where to find designs

The most interesting design parlor may be right inside your home. Look around! You will be surprised to see how many wooden objects there are in your home. Even more amazing will be how many things you can redecorate. You can change a previously drab piece into something fantastic with a bit of pyrographic art. To give you a wide range of ideas of what different objects have to offer, let us go into specific items and how they can inspire a beautiful pyrography design or pattern.

Vegetation and trees

Vegetation and trees make simple yet beautiful options for practice.

Trees have a general line design to them. The other easy design in nature is the leaf. To burn a leaf, or a tree outline, you need to capture the line outline of each. One of the best skills you will gain when burning a tree, a leaf, or any other piece of plant life is spinning in the medium, rather than spinning your drawing hand. In pyrography, always maintain your hand in the same general position, but move your medium around.

Wood patterns and grains

If we're still in nature as your source of inspiration, there are tons of woods with really beautiful grains. Take either photos or pieces of wood and practice the line art to develop the wood grain on your test piece of wood. Wood grains give you very good training for line-based shading skills. Since the grain does not repeat, but rather follows its own unique path, you will also get good practice for making curved lines.

Animal Paws

Animal paws and little feet are composed of a shape with curves and a set of circles. To capture the different objects in the image will give you a good feel of what you can do in depicting different size lines. You can also practice shading in the paw images. You may also pick animal and baby paw designs at your craft shop. Practice transferring the design from the art paper to the wood medium.

Fruit baskets

Fruit baskets and bunches of fruits are a merger of lines and circles and will give you great practice. You can also add depth to your image by adding one of the shading techniques that you want to go over. Fruit designs are also a nice addition to household items. Think about that boring wooden tray or the wooden spoons. Now you can start creating real art that you can put on display.

Festivals and celebrations

Festivals and celebrations provide great opportunities to practice.

All celebrations, especially religious celebrations, will produce amazing pieces that you can use as inspiration for different types of art. You will find the use of circles, strong lines, sharp lines, and all other types of basic images. Practice a new shading skill you had not worked with before, pushing yourself and your boundaries a little more with each new piece. You can use these later as gifts or decorative pieces in your home.

Animals with two-tone designs

To push your art boundaries a bit more strongly, look for designs with animals as the subject. These can be two-tone animals at the beginning. A cow with black and white markings, a dolphin, a possum, etc. What you are looking for is the fur, the feet, as well as the images on the fur or skin. These will give you excellent ways to start capturing eyes and the nuances of the face.

While discussing art-worthy animals, or insects in this case, we cannot miss a mention of the butterfly. A butterfly has more line art potential and a bit more intricate design to make it more of a challenge to move from paper to wood. It is a fun creature to capture.

Cartoon characters

From modern-day cartoon characters to older cartoon characters, there is no end to the inspiring line art you may derive from this genre. Cartoon characters are also an excellent way to train yourself with illustrating clothes, facial features, and hair with your pyrography tools. Now your craft is becoming more fun and more universal. Practice putting the art forms on slightly larger pieces that will have more texture and shading.

The more attractive thing about cartoon characters is you can practice two-tone pieces. One side in the lightest shading and the other parts or aspects in the darkest shading. These are excellent pieces to bring out the contrast and depth with just one pen tip.

Lettering

Lettering, as in all art, is fundamental to getting a wide range of pieces in pyrography. You can start by creating block letters and then go to the fancier fonts that have curves and shadings. There is no limit to what you can do with letters. You can start with a piece where you only transfer the word outline and fill that in using different shading techniques.

You can take your practice sessions further by making a word that is precious to you in big block letters. Then use each letter to practice a different shading technique. In that way, the art you develop will not only have meaning, but will also give you a good point of reference to remember which technique you enjoyed the most.

Take this method further by making name plaques for important people in your life. You can start with initials if you feel the full name is too daunting. Place that in a different medium. Wooden mugs, key holders, coasters, and all sorts of keepsakes that you can use as gifts that people will treasure. Now you are sharing your art in ways where you won't be afraid that your technique will be judged adversely, if that was something that concerned you. No one is judgmental about their name!

Machinery and equipment

Machinery and equipment enables you to practice working with long lines.

Most vehicles, machines, and equipment, especially building equipment, are a combination of strong lines and circles. These items make for perfect pieces to carry out your art. Take a lawnmower. It has a lot of detail. The handles, the wheels, and its entire structure, all of it provides a fantastic training ground for illustration. Stretch your idea a little bit and try working the design in the thinnest of lines to try out how your wood burning pens will take thin lines.

Machines are also an excellent way to start capturing the 3D feel of things. You can practice creating depth so that your machine is not only a line art. You can add other aspects such as grass to your image to practice the technique with longer lines. The importance of this is to make sure you can make a line with the same consistency across a long path.

Household items

Do not limit your machinery ideas to just the outdoors - go indoors, too. The kitchen and other areas in the house have all sorts of delightful items you can turn into a great piece of art. Let us look at just a few possibilities: picture frames, wall art, notices.

Let us move over to surfaces and look at tables. Are there coasters, trays, flower pots? Move over to the kitchen and think of wooden spoons or magnetic reminders to put on the fridge. As you look around the house, there are tons of inspiring things you can turn into amazing pieces using a pyrography design.

Current trends and sacred art

Sacred art motifs are usually very intricate and have many geometrical shapes placed together. This will give your pen a good test run. Have fun with it and see how curves and different pens behave as you copy this type of art.

The Cosmos, the Planets, the Stars

One of the best things about getting the planetary orbs, the skies, and the stars in your wood burning repertoire is the opportunity to do expansive segments in a darker shade. You can leave out other less dense areas to capture a continent, as an example. If you have a black sky, burn it in and leave the stars in the lighter shades of the wood. There is a lot of detail to capture in this type of work.

Start from the easier pieces and work your way into the more complex pieces if this feels like a level of detail you want to go into. Roads and forests are also an addition you can make to these kinds of sprawling pieces. It will give you practice in presenting a large area on your medium in different styles.

Where to source your designs

In these modern times, the best place to start looking for wonderful designs and ideas is online. There are plenty of sites with "free pyrography artworks" that you can download and replicate. Remember to check if the art has a copyright label to it. There are many pyrography artists that have produced incredible pieces and their work is online. These can serve as a great source of inspiration and a reminder of the potential in the new craft you are getting into.

Do not hesitate to visit places that inspire. Websites such as Pinterest and Reddit are rich in ideas, inspiration, and things you absolutely must try. Also, purchase designs. Friends will also inspire you. Join groups that attract pyrography enthusiasts on social media. Their ideas will help you expand your reach.

Pick up books with illustrations, find content on YouTube. Most of all, practice! Develop an eye for pyrography and you will start seeing options and designs you could try in all sorts of places. Have fun with this. It is art and it should be enjoyable.

Patterns

- Use lettering on gift items, announcements, utensils, accessories, and on larger pieces.

- Use images on pieces of jewelry such as earrings, brooches, and bangles.

- Turn ornaments such as crosses and various symbols into a piece of art using pyrography.

- Make your home a pyrography den. Kitchen, bathroom, car, bedroom, etc. Do not stay only on the smaller pieces; try your hand at the larger pieces. Create a wall masterpiece. Work on an antique table.

- Remember to use many techniques. Work on different pieces. Use patterns, shapes, animals, flowers, scenery, and do not hesitate to pick up a stencil and put it to work.

A word about portraits

Portraits are not normally on the beginner's page. However, if you are already proficient with portraiture in another art form, there is nothing that stops you from trying your hand at doing a portrait using your pyrography pen.

Quick reminder on how to transfer your art to the medium

Step 1: Identify your artwork.

Step 2: Make sure your image is up to scale. It must fit in the exact size as the surface area you will be burning.

Step 3: Mirror your artwork if you are going to use graphite paper.

Step 4: Print your art. Most pyrography artists swear by the laser printer, but any printer will do. Ensure that your ink is dry, so that it does not leave ink marks on your medium. Ink marks are not easy to get rid of on wood.

Step 5: Place your medium in a stable position. Align your artwork facing upwards and tape it in place.

Step 6: Place your graphite paper, inked side to your medium, between the medium and the art. Always leave the extra graphite paper spread away from your drawing hand.

Step 7: Trace your artwork on to your medium. Do not press so hard that you poke a hole, and don't be so gentle that you fail to get a visible image on your medium.

Step 8: Keep checking your work before removing the graphite paper.

Chapter Summary

- In this chapter, we have looked at selecting images to use as designs. It is important to take a deliberate approach. We encourage the reader to choose designs that best allow them to develop contour, tone, and texture in their work.

- With continued practice, you will discover even better ways to combine your shading techniques to full effect. In the chapter, we have delved into areas that are common to all art. These are areas that offer the pyrography artists points of inspiration. The inspired artist will not run out of unique ideas to put different techniques into practical effect.

- This chapter should show the reader that practice does not have to be without an aim. You can turn your practice pieces into beautiful artworks for other uses, such as gifts and decorations. Finally, we have made suggestions on where the reader can source new ideas and designs. You will also find insights on portraits in pyrography and where they fit into the scheme of things for the beginner.

In the next chapter, we will discuss:

- Art principles and their connection with pyrography.

- If you are already skilled in another art form, you will enjoy this chapter.

CHAPTER NINE

ARTISTIC PRINCIPLES USED IN PYROGRAPHY

When one endeavors to create in a new artistic medium, there are some basic principles to keep in mind. These transcend any single form of art, and help better your skill in any medium and in any art form. If you are already confident in your knowledge regarding the underlying fundamentals of art, you may choose to skip this chapter. However, there is always something to be learned, and we aim to discuss some interesting topics and how they specifically relate to pyrography.

We have already covered the primary skills in pyrography, although we haven't dealt with finishing. We will get to that after this one. This chapter seeks to highlight important elements of art that will also work in pyrography.

Contrast

The first principle is contrast. In art, contrast refers specifically to the weight of dark areas versus that of completely light (untouched media) areas. It also refers to the direct juxtaposition of any two visual elements. Contrast may mean conflicting textures or sudden tonal shifts. We are less interested here in its meaning regarding color, but in other disciplines, it is important.

So what do we mean when we refer to contrast in pyrography? The most striking way in which one can bring contrast into play is obviously through dramatic shifts between dark lines and blank areas of the wood. This can look a little amateurish and 'cheap' if done incorrectly.

A more reliable way to implement contrast is by utilizing shading techniques. Keep in mind that while one usually has the instinct to shade and texture the entire surface of your medium, you will get far better results from practicing restraint and leaving areas untouched. That's particularly true in pyrography, as your medium is already toned to begin with.

The best way to select areas to contain higher contrast is to find your focal point. For example, most designs of animals portray the creature's eyes as a focal point. So you would put a particular emphasis on dramatic contrast in and around the eye area.

One's attention is immediately drawn to areas of high contrast. That could mean you accidentally draw attention away from the intended focal point. In most of the designs you choose, you will have the flexibility to decide on the focal area yourself, and contrast is the best way for you to highlight that which you want emphasized.

Balance

The next principle we look at is balance. This generally refers to the weight distribution of various elements in your artwork. Although it may sound sensible to have a symmetrical and well-balanced final product, this negates any visual tension, which is crucial to any good pyrographic artwork.

The easiest way to achieve optimal balance is to consider how you might naturally break the symmetry in a way that compliments your artwork and brings attention to elements that you would like to highlight. As with all core artistic principles, it is in doing things with intent that you avoid the final product coming across as amateurish.

There are three primary techniques used in art to create balance. The first is symmetry. This is the least effective method. It is also unappealing as you are essentially mirroring your subject, if not always directly, then in the distribution of the weight of the elements within your 'frame.'

This technique should only be used deliberately. There is a degree of shifted symmetry that sees it change into an asymmetric composition. This form of composition is also the most common, as it appears more satisfying to the eye.

Asymmetry is generally combined with another principle called the rule of thirds. This is an imaginary grid that sees the frame broken up into a grid of three blocks across and three down. Where the four lines intersect defines the four points that one may choose from to place the primary focus of your layout.

This layout will always be asymmetrical. It's considered to be the most visually appealing layout, and also the easiest to guide the viewer's eye through your picture. Another principle that ties in with these two key rules of layout is the golden rule, or the backward six, as it is often called. This principle creates a deliberate placement of elements of a design to accommodate the way that the eye generally follows an artwork. The spiraling line constituting the six indicates the best 'path' on which to place elements in your pyrography design, with the overlapping of the grid focal point on the upper right-hand side making the best placement for your primary subject.

It is worth noting that this layout is best suited to those whose language is read and written from right to left starting on the upper right-hand side of the page. People who are brought up in a language that is written from left to right tend to follow an exact reversal of this layout.

The final artistic principle that applies to pyrography is visual tension. This is the principle of creating life-like dynamism in an image. If your design is a bird perched on a branch, blankly staring at nothing, your final image will seem lifeless.

Adding an intent focus, or just an additional element to the image, can breathe life into the 'narrative.' It helps create a final product that captures attention and piques the viewer's interest. Those who start out practicing artistic techniques will quite likely find that people go from commenting, 'Oh, that's nice,' to actually engaging with the art as you bring in more visual tension.

Keep in mind that art is not a strict science. But it is useful to learn the rules before you decide to break them. A fundamental understanding of these principles will allow you more freedom to create representations of designs that better reflect your vision.

Important points

We have gone through the basics of the most important artistic principles and how to make use of them to improve the quality of your work. We have looked at contrast and the role it plays in bringing attention to the focal point. We've also discussed symmetry and asymmetry and touched on why asymmetry is the more popular layout. We've considered visual tension and the importance of bringing life into your final artwork.

Up to this point in the book, we have discussed how to build your pyrography skill with the right tools, the right medium choices, how to be safe, and, finally, how to map your art.

What to Remember

Always think safety first

Pyrography is "burning with fire." The two words, "burning" and "fire," should be red flags at all times. The pyrography tool does burn. So the first thing to keep in mind is to always think about pyrography the same way you think about fire in the kitchen. Safety must be uppermost in your mind.

Know your pens and what they can do

Once you know your pens and have prepared both your wood and your workspace, the next step would be to choose a suitable design. Whilst choosing a beautiful and complex design with various elements may be tempting, it is recommended that you choose strategically according to the skill sets required to carry out a design. The design is what will help you choose the pen tip or the art technique that will work for the particular piece.

Practice your techniques

You do not want to ruin a good piece of wood. To make sure you get your art right, choose practice pieces of wood to practice your technique. You want to go over each technique methodically before dedicating time and effort to a design that requires a combination of each. The best place to start, as with sketching, is your line work. You want your first designs to be predominantly an exercise in mastering this skill.

Master how to make your lines

Creating the outline is a significant step and comes long before you start burning. To begin with, transfer the artwork and then start burning with a very basic outline. You could do an image search for simple line work designs. Adult coloring books are a good source of fantastic designs to work with. In this process, you will focus only on learning to create uniform lines on your pyrographic medium.

Master one skill to give you pen tip practice

To master lines, for instance, you will primarily use your solid-point burner. As your line work skill improves, your challenge will be to continuously do finer detailed line work, improving on your abilities all the time.

Once you are quite comfortable with line work and have done a number of complete projects to hone your ability, you may want to move on to shading as your next skill. This is a far more challenging skill to learn. It depends on practical skill but also on an aptitude similar to that of sketch shading.

Chapter Summary

- In this chapter, we looked at the thought process of the pyrography artist. The focus is on what happens when one endeavors to create art in a new medium. We've expanded the ideas from out of the artistic principles that already exist. From that foundation, we draw on the basic artistic principles to keep in mind when developing pyrography.

- The main aim of this chapter is to bring harmony between pyrography and other forms of art. The principles discussed transcend art forms. With this information at the back of the reader's mind, the pyrographic artist will find points of harmony between what they are developing and what is happening in other art they encounter.

- We've outlined important elements of art that will also work in pyrography, especially in selecting the designs and developing a final work. The purpose of these elements is to harmonize the pyrography artwork to the way art is viewed. This chapter shows you the principles that will guide your technique and help you achieve the results you desire.

In the next chapter, we will look at:

- Methods in applying finish to your pyrography artwork.

CHAPTER TEN

METHODS TO APPLYING FINISH

In this chapter, we will look at methods to finish your pyrography artwork. Specifically, we will look at wood sealants. We will discuss what works best for different types of media and artwork.

Burn before adding color

Let us start on a high note with one of the most common newbie mistakes; adding color to your work and then burning your art. You may add color to your art if you so wish. Adding color to a pyrography artwork has no negative effects. You can create your design in such a way as to provide room to add color. Also, wood burning is generally sepia; so, if you want your work to be unique it is not unusual to add color to the finished product. But the sequence is vital. First complete the burning and then add the color. Why is this important?

Color, more often than not, is chemically based. Therefore you will be burning chemicals. The fumes from these could be toxic, smelly, and even potentially unsafe. These are important factors to keep in mind.

So go ahead and knock yourself out with gold stains and other art forms to spice up your pyrography, but always remember that the pyrography comes first and then the other additives. "Burn before glam."

Why apply finish to your art?

Art finishes ensure the work lasts longer. The pyrography burns, as in most other methods of art, will fade in time. Although pyrography will not fade as quickly as most other art methods such as paint and pencil, it is still a good idea to give that smooth and shiny finish to your work.

It also protects the wood from parasites, the elements, carbon, and any other toxic fumes that could be in the air. If your art piece will be subjected to the occasional wash, as would happen with a wooden tray, then the burn will fade in time.

Finished pieces of art tend to be hardier. It makes the wood stronger and prevents cracks, breakages, and damage from stains and spills. Finish provides a barrier from the changes in temperatures and moisture in the air. Wood loses and absorbs water from out of the atmosphere. A finish layer protects the art by keeping the moisture levels constant.

Finishing protects your art from general weathering as well as damage in the course of human use of the art. Fingerprints on pieces that are handled will often damage the wood and leave blotches. Art on a wall as an art piece is sturdier if it is finished and looks brighter for longer.

With that understanding, let us get right into what finishes you can work with and how to apply them.

Spray or paint? That is the question!

One of the most common questions that new pyrography art students will ask is what is the best method to use to finish their work. Should you use a spray painter or a brush to apply finishing?

As a general guideline, spraying finish is a quick and easy way to seal a wood burning piece. The spray will not disturb the color; the sealer is applied through an aerosol spray. This is in comparison to brush strokes that can disturb the color and even destroy the piece of art.

To make an informed decision, there are two primary considerations right off the top.

The first is your budget. Spray finishes tend to be costlier than brush-on finishes. The second consideration is the number of pieces you will be regularly finishing. If you are going to be doing a lot, then spray painting is more time-efficient. Having said that, keep in mind that gallon finishes will offer you a better price on volume. Therefore, it will not be too costly.

Spray painting your finish is great for both large and small projects. For the smaller projects, you get more on the detail when using a spray painter.

Next, we will look at specific scenarios and the choices you have.

Finish is an extra layer on your artwork. If you have added color to your art, then use a spray painter on your first application of finish. Brush bristles and the physical act of painting will scrape against the art and distort the paint. That will damage the art quality.

Choose a finish based on the type of wood you've used. The finishes that add a hue to the wood will make the grains on the wood really stand out. This will affect the overall presentation of your pyrography image. If your wood does not have too much grain on it, then you want to decide if you want the hue or not. Sometimes the hue is really cool, sometimes not so much.

Finish application technique

Your art is complete, and you now want to apply the finisher. What finish should you use? This is an important question as the finish will affect your final product. Some argue that finishing products are not necessary, but for the reasons above, you can decide whether to apply a coat of finish to your art or not.

We will delve into the various types of finishes, but let us take a moment to go through the application techniques and principles.

117

A significant element to all the finishes you will use is applying the finish on all surfaces of the art, including the sides. The side of the wood is also part of the art. It will give your work a beautiful look if the entire top and sides are the same glossy look.

There is a technique to applying finish. Do it in three steps:

- Depending on the finish you're using, dilute it to give it an even application on the first layer. This is primarily relevant for the finishes that are not oil-based.

IMPORTANT: always read the application instructions on the finish.

Once the first layer is dry, buffer it slightly with the finest grit sandpaper to give it a slightly rough feel. This is a very gentle sanding. It will enable the first coat of finish to bond properly with the next coat.

Apply the next two coats of finish, giving enough time with each application to allow it to dry. Always set aside at least a day for application of finish. Give at least three, and up to six hours, between applications.

All finishes have a curing period. Read the label to identify how long the finish you have is going to take to cure. The range is between 30 days to 60 days.

Never dip an application brush into the finish. Pour out some finish into an old tin and use that portion to work with. The brush comes into contact with the wood of your art. The brush will absorb particles, or some contaminant, and this will affect the whole batch of finish. It will give your finish a shorter shelf life. To avoid contamination, use only the finish you need in a side container. Make sure you shut the larger container tight. If it is left open, the finish starts to dry over time.

Always clean your brushes thoroughly with thinner after each application. Leave them out to dry. For some finishes, you may have to replace the brushes altogether.

Apply finish in a room at medium temperature. Most finishes set better when warm (not hot), and cold temperatures may impair the result. You want the workspace you are using to be warm, as well as the wood itself. This helps the final product set faster and more uniformly. Various products should have some indication on the label regarding the ideal temperature for the specific product. Do not heat the room artificially unless it is during winter. Just make sure it is room temperature and on the warmer side.

Never mix finishing products. Only use a single product at a time. This is essential because some finishes and varnishes may chemically react to each other. Always read the product information before trying any unique combinations. Most finishes are going to give you the best results when used as directed.

What you need to know before applying finish

When applying a finish, it is always best to do so one layer at a time. Allow each layer to set and dry evenly.

Let us take a deeper look now at the most popular types of finishes commonly used in pyrography.

Lacquer finishes

The first is lacquer. This is a great option for anyone looking for a durable result. Before using it on your substrate, it is important that it's applied with a lacquer thinner first. This is very easy to find, not too costly, and comes in brush-on or spray-on applications.

Because of the strong odor it releases, it is always recommended applying it in a well-ventilated area. While lacquer does age over time, a fact that is definitely important to keep in mind, it is also easy to sand down and reapply.

Oil-based finishes

The next option is oil. This is an umbrella term referring to a number of different types of wood oil products. The oil of your choice is brushed onto the wood, with any excess to be wiped off. After leaving your substrate to set overnight, you may choose to apply a second coat.

Oils are great because they impart new properties to the wood. Mineral oil can withstand high temperatures. It will not discolor or crack even when used on items that will be subjected to heat, such as coasters. It is non-toxic. For this reason, they are ideal for pieces that are going to come in contact with food and with human skin. Examples are kitchen cutting boards and cooking spoons. Other popular oils for use in pyrography include lemon, walnut, tung, and Danish oil.

Shellac

Shellac is a finish made from the secretions of the female Lac bug. It is thought to be safe as it contains no harsh chemicals. It is tagged as the only bio-friendly finish on the market. The finish is brushed on in thin layers, setting in around an hour, after which another coat may be applied. The important thing to keep in mind about Shellac is that it discolors in proximity to heat, hence it is not ideal for use on works that will be kept near indoor heating or in a kitchen. It also does not have a strong odor. It can thus be used on indoor furniture and other household items.

Polyurethane

One of the most common finishes for pyrography is polyurethane. This product can be found as a spray or as a viscous brush-on fluid. It comes in different versions, including high-gloss, gloss, and matte. It is available in water-based and oil-based options.

The finish does tend to give wood a slightly yellow tint. It is best to apply polyurethane in a thin coat. After allowing it to dry for eight to twelve hours, gently sand it down. You may choose to repeat this process two to three times.

Wax

Paste wax is a very flexible finishing option. It leaves the substrate glossy. Wax is a fantastic option for smaller items that need more attention to detail. It is simple to apply.

Using a clean cloth to apply a modest amount to the wood, rub it into the wood in a consistent circular motion. Make sure you spread the wax evenly on the top and the sides of the piece of art. Once you have covered the whole artwork, leave it to dry.

Once dry, buff the surface into a sheen. You can then repeat this by adding another layer. Keep the wax to a minimum, much as you would if brushing shoes. Too much wax will ruin the final product, leaving it looking cloudy.

Chapter Summary

- In this chapter, we have looked at methods to finish your pyrography artwork. We have specifically narrowed the discussion on finishing to wood sealants and finishes that will work in wood burning. The chapter discusses the application methods that are available. For pyrography, we've considered when you should spray your finish and when you should apply finish with a brush.

- How do you make sure your finish does not distort the work you have spent so much effort to perfect? We have discussed what works best for different types of wood and what you should look out for on the label when buying.

- Finally, we have recommended practical application skills on how to apply finish. There is also a list of products that you will find in the market. The chapter looks at an important issue for those that intend to develop household items - what finishes are toxic and which ones are food-friendly. How does the pyrography artist identify the difference?

In the next chapter, we will look at:

- Common problems that beginners face and suggestions for troubleshooting techniques.

CHAPTER ELEVEN

TROUBLESHOOTING

We have come to the end of our examination of the techniques of pyrography. In this chapter, we will help you troubleshoot common problems that you may face as you begin your journey. We've divided the trouble spots in headings for easier reference. Let us get right into it.

The price tags are intimidating:

This is a common challenge for most beginners. Go with what you can afford. You will make quite a series of burnt pieces and practice runs that did not turn out right, so the pricier items will just bring financial pain into what should be fun. Once you have got the feel of things, then you can reach for the pricier options.

The most important thing to look out for in a wood burner is a temperature-adjust dial. Also, look for a burner with at least one of the three tips; the writer, the skew, and the shader. The other fancier pieces and kits that come with tons of other things are not necessary when starting to learn the skill.

Choking on the smoke

There could be several things happening. First, how is your ventilation? Are you in a well-ventilated area? If yes, then make sure the windows are open. If not, re-plan your work area so that you are in a well-ventilated space.

Check your fan if you have one. What direction is your fan facing in relation to the window or the ventilation? If your fan is facing inwards, then it is drawing the smoke towards you. Fix the direction of the fan so that it is blowing the smoke away from you.

If these two are in place and you are still choking on the fumes, you could be working on wood that has a finish. Sand the wood and remove all the finish. Most finishes are chemical-based and thus emit toxic fumes. These are not safe for inhalation.

QUICK TIP: there are smoke-capture gadgets that will draw the smoke away from you. These are great if you cannot find a well-ventilated area to work in.

Image transfer techniques

It will be super-helpful if you have a printer with you. All of us have computers, but a printer will be a good addition to your office or pyrography studio. This will come in very handy when you are developing your design transfer pieces.

Clearing dust gathered as you correct mistakes

Most of the mistake-clearing techniques will create a fine dust. To clean your work as you go, have a small piece of soft cloth to keep swiping at the area as you proceed.

Trouble when using your wood burner

When you do not get the line you want, change your pen tip. The writer pen tip is best for really thin lines. As you practice, it will also work for thin curved lines too. As you get to areas that need a wider line, move to the writer with a wider ball-point tip and other shaders, and to fill in your spaces, turn more to the skews. If you are having a problem with developing smooth circles, work with the writer a lot more; it has a more rounded pen tip and will be smoother.

Troubleshooting lines

Getting a blob at the beginning and end of the line. This is because the pen was already hot before placing it on your wood. If you stall at the beginning and on touching the wood, it will burn deeper. The temperature of the nib will cool somewhat as you continue the line. Thus, the line will become softer as you continue to draw. At the end of the line, the blob appears when you stop before lifting the pen off the wood. To solve this problem, refine your technique so that your pen is in constant motion on touching the wood and in motion as you lift it off the wood.

Your line is darker than you desire

This happens when your pen is hotter than it should have been for the tone you wanted to achieve. You may use an ink eraser if the burn was not too dark. The other tool you can pick up is the spot sander, also called the fiberglass eraser. It is highly abrasive and will sand off the darkened parts. Be very gentle using it because its abrasive edge can put a hole in your medium. In addition, you cannot use it for expansive sections.

Another tool that you can use to correct mistakes over larger areas, especially if the burning is darker than you intended, is the box cutter. A surgical blade in a holder will also work. A precision cutter will also serve the purpose. Scrape off the darkened wood gently. Use the wider edge of the blade to create a scraping motion, not a cutting motion. A cutting motion will create a groove in your work.

You can achieve the same scraping effect with fine grit sandpaper. The main task is to be gentle and to keep the scraping gentle so that it only removes the top film of color.

If you are still working on your technique, mistakes are all a part of learning. A skill to learn is to use low heat on your burner. Get the lighter shades in first. Slowly build up your heat to get the exact tone you want.

Do not get too distressed about mistakes. As you refine your technique, you may even find creative ways to turn your "mistake" into part of your art. You can introduce a new aspect to your design using the "mistake" as the launch part. With time, and as you refine your technique, you'll steadily eliminate mistakes altogether.

Grain lines that interfere with your design

When the wood grain lines interfere with your design, there are a number of problems that can occur. To start with, for beginning with pyrography, be careful when choosing your wood. The more visible your grain lines, the more difficult it will be to create art that does not clash with the lines.

The second thing you can do, if you do intend to work with wood that has grain lines, is to work with the grain lines as part of your design. The third thing is to make sure you do not burn with a hot pen enough to make the grain lines evident. If you cannot do any of the above, then lighten the color in the grain line using any of the methods discussed above.

Some grains will create ridges after the work is complete. These may not fill in neatly as you shade and will leave line marks on your final work. To clear these grain lines, remember to sand your paper well at the beginning. Also, remember to spray a little water on your wood, letting it dry, and sanding again with a low grit sandpaper. This removes most of the lines.

In some woods, the grain lines will still show. To clear these, choose your writer pen tip and on low heat. Go over the grain line, gently increasing the shade in the line until it looks like the rest of the burnt art.

Picking up the wrong tip

It is possible to pick up the wrong tip to do something that it will not do. If it is sharp and you are pressing too hard, it will not create a design. It will cut through the wood and leave a line-burn. It will also cut and create a ridge in the wood. Pressing too hard will make it nearly impossible for you to make a curve or even a circle. So the pen tip for creating lines is one with a bit of form on the edge.

This will be your shader and not your writer. Refer to the chapter on pen tips for the tips with rounded writing tips. If you try and push the wrong pen tip too hard, you will probably end up with a broken tip. The trick is the pen tip should flow along on the surface without resistance.

Getting bumpy lines along the wood grain

This is another issue about technique. When you are getting a bumpy consistency or your pen keeps bumping along, then there is a problem. It means you are applying too much pressure - your pen tip is snagging on the wood grain. You will need to lighten up the pressure to get a smoother and straighter line.

Pausing mid-stroke

When you pause or hesitate when you are burning, that section is going to burn too long. You will get a blotch or a mark that is heavier than you wanted. The technique for getting a smooth and even burn consistency is to train your hand to move at the same pace over the burn area. This will be particularly important when you are shading. If you shade too slow and then too fast on the same heat, you will get a different shade.

What if you have lightened the pressure but are still getting a bumpy burn?

The chances are you are working against the wood grain. For the easiest work, flow along the path of the wood grain. Working against the grain will give you a harder time getting the lines and shapes you want.

The final work has dents that shouldn't be there

The idea behind wood burning is not to cut into the wood; it is to pass a flame over the wood. So you need to regard it as though you were passing your wood burner over your hand to see if it's hot. You wouldn't touch your hand. You would pass it about an inch above your hand. That is the same general motion you will need to master with your pen. In wood burning, you do put pressure on the wood. It is the temperature of the burner that makes the difference, not the pressure.

A common mistake is to use the wood burning tip as you would a pencil or a cutting tool. The right way is to apply just enough pressure. Light pressure allows you to gain control over your pen and develop graceful strokes that make a difference as you go. When you master a lighter weight on the pen tip, you will also work much faster since the glide will be smoother.

The best part of mastering the low-pressure technique in holding your burning tool is that you minimize the number of errors and accidental burns. Finally, and really importantly, too much pressure can and will break your wood burning tips. So go easy on how hard you press.

You want to make a wider curved line

If you want to achieve a curved line that turns sharply to almost a circle, the writing tip might be a bit clumsy. Change your tip to a writing tip. If you want a thinner line than you can get with a writing tip, use the sharp pointy tip of a shader to achieve the sharp line. Keep in mind that the flat end of a shader is for shading and will not give you a line.

When image transfer is giving you a headache

So what comes after the other in starting your project? Once you have identified your piece of wood and your design, the next step is to get our design onto your wood as a reference. That can be easily achieved by using a graphite or carbon transfer sheet.

Look through the chapter on artistic principles discussed earlier. They will apply here. We will not go through each one again where it's applicable in our preparation.

132

The nice thing about transferring your art is that some transfer sheets can be put through a printer (confirm this before trying, though), meaning you can print your design directly onto the sheet and transfer that to your wood without needing to redraw it.

Should you prefer a more hands-on approach, you may decide to draw the design, either on transfer or directly onto the wood. Should you choose the latter, it is vital that you take great care not to create any indentation with your pencil. A good rule of thumb is to use transfer media on softwood, while either approach will work for harder types of wood. It is also important that the pencil you use should not be sharp; even hardwood can be damaged in this way. Take your time with this step; the better the reference, the better the final artwork should be.

Finally, some people do opt for a projector, and although many swear by it, it tends to make the image warp too easily if the alignment isn't just right. Regardless of which method you choose, you will quickly run into the biggest challenge of setting up your reference images.

When working with typography is not going well

Transferring typography media generally does not do well when it comes to shading, and you are more likely to end up with an unworkable smudged mess. There are two ways in which pyrography artists solve this problem. You will choose one that will appeal to your personal preference, so do try each at least once.

The first method is to use a very light pencil (2H-4H) and create reference shading in the form of hatching through transfer media. The second option is to do it freehand directly on your substrate. That will most likely be decided by your level of comfort with normal sketching.

There is an altogether more challenging aspect to preparing your reference - that of adding letters to your design.

The problem is this: anyone who has seen a horse knows how a horse looks in a general sense. When you do a rendition of a horse in your artwork, it doesn't matter if the eyes are a little bigger or the posture slightly slanted compared to your reference. That's because these are all attributes a real horse might have. So, the suspension of disbelief isn't broken.

Typography does not offer any such leniency. A small detail out of place in a letter is extremely noticeable when compared to correctly done versions of that same letter. The best way to go about it is to categorize the different techniques into different scenarios. Consider the text you have in mind. It is not as simple as using a printed-out sheet with the wording you want to burn and then tracing it to your substrate.

As mentioned, small deviations from a design, whether intentional or accidental, are not as noticeable in an image. While designing your text to scale on a computer, using something like Coral Draw is definitely helpful, and a reference is clearly a useful thing to have so that you can focus on steady and fluent line work.

- **Freehand Writing**

The first way one might go about it is to have a go at freehand writing. This is not recommended for anyone who has untidy handwriting. It is very much a skill that depends on your aptitude for fine detail and tidy forms.

- **Using script fonts**

It is best to start off with script fonts, using either a transfer reference on your wood or having a print-out in clear view for freehand work. Script- and decorative fonts have more flamboyant details that hide deviation quite well.

While the steady hand of a calligrapher may manage impressive freehand results, you may need to invest in pyrography stamp sets if your handwriting is more suggestive of medical school! These are not too expensive to come by, although they are rather tedious to work with.

This approach involves replacing the nib to that of the specific letter, waiting for it to heat up to the correct temperature, and, using a metal ruler, aligning it to the sentence you are working on. By using only this technique, you are limiting your options as far as variety; hence, it is a good idea to practice freehand typography.

In terms of getting started with our first project, one must factor typography into the equation and be sure to have a plan as to how you are going to approach the challenge.

Working with mistakes in typography

Let us now move on and get to the actual 'pyro' in pyrography. We start by burning our outlines into the wood. The first time you do this, you are going to end up with undesirable results. That's because one needs to practice getting the weight and tone exactly so. 'Exactly so' will differ from one design to another.

This first step to creating your own pyrography artwork will serve more as a learning experience. Making mistakes is normal. It is good to get an idea of what to do and what not to do and this is best realized in practice.

Next, ignoring any mistakes you may have made, it is time to start working on shading. It is worth noting that there is nothing wrong with delaying shading should you prefer to get comfortable first with the line work.

There are two primary methods by which to go about shading, both equally valid, which are up to personal preference. Most artists prefer starting with the dark areas of shading and lightening the shade up as they work inward. Others prefer composite shading. That's where one does the entire shaded area in the lightest tone that you will be using, and then add darker shades toward the darkest point of the intended shadow. This is again a case where you will benefit from trying both so that you are certain you are working in such a way as is comfortable.

Both of the above-mentioned methods apply to all forms of shading. We will not go into them again, but hatching and stippling will be approached in much the same way.

While working on your shading, you need to keep the overall tone in mind. That tends to be another mistake we all make when starting out; going too dark in certain areas, then having to darken all the shading in the artwork to repair the contours of the design. Our exercise for shading should come in as a great help in avoiding this problem.

Adjusting to typography mistakes

A rather good bit of advice to take heed of is to stop and step back when you do make a mistake. The majority of ruined pyrography works are caused by hastily trying to cover up mistakes. Step back and consider the different techniques at your disposal and choose the approach that requires the least possible deviation from the original design. It is also important that one not deviate from the design on purpose, at least not when starting out.

Ignoring mistakes where possible, it is now time to use the finishing product of your choice as directed in the previous chapter. The combination of the type of wood and type of finish should be the catalyst that rounds out your artwork.

Continue practicing in this way. As with all skills, it does require practice. Because burning is a less forgiving media than painting or sketching, there are bound to be mistakes. You are using this time to exercise your skill and develop familiarity with the tools of the trade.

Pen tips are black and have misshaped edges: clean your pen tips

Dirty pen tips are going to make your burning that much more difficult. The dirt on pen tips comes from gathering carbon as you burn. This is a type of soot. Your pen tips are due for cleaning if they are blackened, are usually smooth but now are bumping along, and if they are smudging the lines.

Solution. Take a bit of sandpaper and sand the edges. If that does not work, you can have them professionally cleaned. It is called polishing. There are specific scouring pads for pen tips in certain kits, so check out if yours is one of them. Clean pen tips will always give you better and cleaner lines, so schedule your cleaning after a set time to maintain the edges. If you are really good with tools, you can risk using a razor edge to scrape off the carbon.

Pen tip broke inside burner

Depending on how far in the break is, there are a number of things you can do if your pen tip has broken inside your burner. The first is to switch off the burner and unplug it. Do not try and work on it when it is hot and certainly not when it is plugged in.

Once it is cool, check if you can pull the pen tip out with a pair of pliers. If it has a screw tip, that will need a bit more skill. Here is a quick tutorial. Try and see if you can find a way to make the tip stuck inside longer. You can do this with a bit of glue attached to a piece of wood or metal you do not need. Wait for it to dry and twist it out.

Be careful with this, as you can glue it in instead of removing the tip. If this idea does not work for you, then go to the next alternative, which is to speak with the supplier. Sometimes your burner can still be salvaged.

If your burner will not work

If your burner suddenly does not work, check the electrical supply. If the electrical current is flowing well, but the burner is still not heating, check if the nibs are too coated over with carbon. This, by the way, slows you down tremendously, so always aim at working with clean pen tips. If that is not the case, then there could be a problem with the burner.

Chapter Summary

- You get to the market and the price tags are intimidating; what do you do? Why is your working area so smoky? What can you do? My image transfer techniques need refining; what can I do? There is fine dust as I work, how can I clear it? Is your wood burner difficult to work with? We've discussed some solutions you might want to look at.

- My lines are rough and jagged? My lines are too dark? The grain lines are interfering with my design work? Are the lines bumpy along the wood grain? I can't seem to get the right tip to do what I want it to do? I lightened the pressure on my pen tip but I am still getting a bumpy burn? My final work has dents that shouldn't be there? I want to make a wider curve? Image transfer is still giving me a headache?

- My typography work is not going well, what can I do? My pen tips are black and have misshaped edges; what could be the problem? My pen tip broke inside my burner, what can I do? My burner is not working, why?

- These are all problems that can occur, and we've included a range of ideas and suggestions to correct most of these mistakes in typography.

In the next chapter, we will discuss:

- Mastering artistic self-expression through pyrography.

CHAPTER TWELVE

MASTERING SELF-EXPRESSION THROUGH PYROGRAPHY

Self-expression is the primary reason most of us take up an art form. While tracing images directly is a fantastic way to learn, there is so much more available to the budding enthusiast. While this may not seem as important as the practicalities of pyrography, it will likely be what defines whether you stick to it or become bored. A quick online search will bring up so many hits of people complaining that they get bored with all the tracing, and, unfortunately, it would seem that the true scope and flexibility of the art form is lost on many. But it is a fully-fledged mode of art in its own right.

As your skill develops with practice, you will likely find yourself gradually bringing your personal flair into your projects. This is not merely an idiosyncrasy; it is the artist within utilizing new skills to create something unique to you.

The standard misconceptions about pyrography may also lie in the way that the art form is represented. Many people believe that pictures of deer and tigers pretty much account for the entire craft. The truth, of course, is that there are very few limits, certainly no more than you would find in pencil or charcoal sketching.

Bring your inner artist out to play

Every skill relating to sketching has an equivalence in pyrography. That's why practicing, or refining your drawing skills, is an excellent way to improve your pyrography. While the tools and processes may differ, the logic remains consistent in both disciplines.

That is not to compare the two. Those who are experienced in both often say they find pyrography the more challenging but also the more rewarding. It is inarguable that the one helps define your inner artist in terms of the other.

A good way to find this inner artist is by imitation. It may sound the exact opposite of being original, but art school students are taught to do the same. Human beings are imitative creatures. Sometimes we need to replicate other work we admire and then, gradually, our own voice emerges. You first recreate famous works, interpreted in your medium. Later, you use the skills you pick up to define your own style - your unique artistic fingerprint.

This extends to your subject of choice. If you are intent on recreating scenes from nature in your pyrography work, choose images of nature as your references. Start simple with designs you might find in an adult coloring book.

As your skill improves steadily, guide your practice to styles you like most in the work of others. This kind of practice will instill an almost instinctive understanding of your subject, and allows you to take more liberties in your reproduction of various works.

There are people who focus almost completely on cats as subjects, and they will attest to this sort of intuitive effect of finding a theme. It is as though you just know the proportions and contours of the object or scene you have become so familiar with.

That's not to say that you should limit yourself. It is just a good idea to be familiar with the types of subjects you want to recreate. This brings us to our primary topic for this chapter. Creating your own original artwork.

You will find that most of the historic art movements offer the opportunity to develop skills and reinterpretations that will apply to wood as a substrate. It is a good idea to go through the different styles and most popular works from the many historic influences. They may end up becoming a part of your aesthetic.

Do not hesitate to try something different

There are a couple of options. We will skip over the first, that of freehand pyrography from memory; this is not a common skill that many people possess. Instead, we will look at creating our own references. The easiest way would be to sketch your designs from a reference or multiple references, and use the final sketch along with a transfer medium to apply it to your substrate.

Another option, one that those familiar with digital design software like Illustrator and Coral Draw, would prefer, is going all digital. That does present two challenges. Anyone familiar with these programs will know that you use vector shapes to create and manipulate your work. The problem is that shading and vectors make for a famously poor combination. It is not impossible, but it is very time-consuming and easy to get wrong. This approach should be reserved for those who are confident in their understanding of how vector art works.

As you continue to develop your technique and gradually bring more of what you like into play, you will find that your artistic style naturally emerges.

A look into styles that inspire new ideas

To further expand, let us consider art styles that are appropriate to pyrography. You will find that the great artistic movements throughout history have relevance to wood burning.

Cubism

Cubism is one such movement that one would not immediately associate with pyrography, but there are stunning examples of interpretations of the work of Picasso and other artists famous for their contributions to the movement. The ability to control tone and shading makes wood burning a striking media for reinterpreting the works that arose from this era in art history. You will find the same can be said for Constructivism and the great Bauhaus movement.

Art deco often comes across as intended for pyrography when implemented by a skilled artisan. The formularized forms and exaggerated verticality seem almost natural to wood.

Pop art

Pop Art is another example that lends itself to pyrography rather well. Because a lot of the shading is replaced with solid tonal overlays, Pop Art is ideal for practicing flat contouring.

Pointillism

Pointillism is an artistic genre that is well-suited to wood burning. It is also a lot of fun! The dotting technique is particularly suitable for pyrography.

Advancing your self-expression through pyrography

Self-expression is something that we tend to do as a pastime or hobby, but the more advanced techniques, and the overall quality of work produced, demands dedication. As your skill level improves, you will find that the different media at your disposal expands. You need not confine yourself to working exclusively with slats of wood. There are innumerable other ways in which you can use wood burning to create unique and magnificent works. Consider the options that open up to you by expanding your work to furniture. To reach the level where you can confidently work on more complex substrates, you need to be able to use different techniques, pens, and tones with ease. Set goals for yourself and take your pyrography to new heights of self-expression.

Chapter Summary

- Self-expression is the primary reason most of us take up a new art form. While tracing images directly is a fantastic way to learn, there is so much more available to the budding enthusiast. While this may not seem as important as the practicalities of pyrography, it will likely be what defines whether you stick to it or become bored.

- In this chapter, we offered suggestions on how to bring out the inner artist. We've also given the budding pyrography artist ideas on how to find inspiration in the ordinary. Some of the suggestions in this chapter address the use of modern technology. We've included a few ideas on how to utilize wood burning in creative ways that could resonate with you in your environment.

- As a final word, we encourage the individual venturing into this art to be courageous. Like all art forms, there are basic principles and when those are put into effect, they become a unique and beautiful art. It's our hope that this book will inspire you to take wood burning beyond a hobby into a lifestyle.

The next section will serve as a reference document. It covers everything you have learned in this book at a glance. Please use it often until you refine your wood burning skill so that it's become an expression of an amazing and personal art.

SUMMARY

BEGINNER'S TIPS FOR PYROGRAPHY AT A GLANCE

This is a summary chapter that will give you the main highlights of what you need to remember from each chapter in the book.

a) The History And Origins Of Pyrography

Pyrography, or the art of burning or writing with fire, is a modern art form with long roots in history. You can trace pyrography from as far back as humanity's discovery of fire through to working with metals. The earliest and crude forms of pyrography were called poker work. You can trace the beginnings of pyrography as an idea through the development of poker work through various civilizations from Egypt, through Peru, through to China. As we approach the 1900s, we see the development of the platinum pencil. This laid a foundation for shading, a skill that is still very relevant to modern pyrography.

Finally, you will find the history of pyrography well-defined in the development of poker work. The poker, placed in fire and used to emblazon records in the earliest forms of writing, is a clear foundation of what is today known as pyrography.

The modern forms have expanded the media to include leather, canvas, bones, gourds, and other materials. Modern pyrography is largely known as wood burning because it is the most common media in use.

b) Pyrography Tools and Other Supplies

The most important tool in pyrography is the wood burner. It is also referred to as the wood burning pen. A wood burning unit constitutes the pen, which looks much like a soldering iron, the electrical connection on one side, and the pen tip on the other.

There are two main pen tips available on the market: the fixed pen tip, which comes attached to the wood burner and the detachable pen tip. The other item to look out for in a wood burner is the heat regulation system. The ideal wood burner should have a temperature control system that gives you the ability to control how hot or how cold it gets at the touch of a knob or switch of a button.

When buying your first pen, look out for one that gives you a variety of pen tips. The way the pen tips attach to the burner is also significant if you go for the detachable pen tips. The easier they are to remove, the better in the long term. The attached pen tips do give better heat transfer. So you may opt to go for several burners with the fixed pen tip.

Your list of supplies will stretch across several stages of the pyrography work. Materials to prepare the wood for burning, materials to transfer the design on your medium, materials to ensure your working space is safe, and then what you will use for finishing.

The main chapter goes through the various ten tips, gives guidelines on important aspects of wood burning pens, and pen tip handling so that your pens will serve you as long as possible.

You will also have a list of supplies that you will need to start your pyrography project. This list will continue to grow as you refine your knowledge of wood burning.

c) Safety Precautions in the Pyrography Workspace

The most essential thing to keep in mind around pyrography is that it is about working with fire. The pyrography pen can burn very hot. The reader needs to internalize this as early as possible so that they can get into pyrography with safety in mind.

The main aspects of safety include the working surface, smoke and ventilation, moving objects, inflammable materials, especially liquids, your clothes, and the way the tools are stored and how they are kept when you are working.

A major point to emphasize is that under no circumstances should you try to touch the pen tip when the unit is connected to the electrical supply. Also, keep the burner off and unplugged if you move away from your working area. Particularly important is to ensure that you maintain strict safety measures around children and pets.

d) Choosing and Preparing Wood for Pyrography

The first point to note in wood selection for the beginner is to keep their choice to lighter-colored woods. The darker woods will require a lot more skill to bring out the results of the burning. The effort may discourage the beginner. You will find a list of wood types and their advantages in the chapter.

You can source your wood from craft shops, timber and lumber yards, as well as from friends. Always remember to work with wood that is clear of varnish or any other type of finish or paint. You may also do your practice runs on wooden items around the house. To expand your wood sources, think about finding craft shops online and also buying from online shops such as Amazon.

e) How to Prepare Your Wood

Take time to think about your clothes as a pyrography artist. You will be working with fire. You will need sanding materials as well as a way to collect the dust that accumulates when you sand your piece of wood. If you prepare more than one piece of wood, plan to do it all at once.

Make sure your working surface is clear of moveable things that can accidentally trigger an accident. We have discussed methods of using your sandpaper and your sander if you have one.

The other aspect of preparing your wood is to transfer the design to the wood. You may use graphite or transfer paper or carbon paper. If you do not have either of the two, find out how to use a pencil to achieve similar results. In the chapter, we give you a view that demystifies pyrography and makes it an art form they can launch with ease.

f) Choosing a Pen Tip and Technique

The three major pen tip types in pyrography pens are the shader, the skew, and the writer. Each does something slightly different. The shader, shades. The writer makes it easy to achieve the same kind of effect you would with a pen. The skew straddles both tasks.

Your pen will give you the best results if you control your temperature and keep the pressure off your pen. Do not press down on your pen. That is not where the magic happens. The magic happens with the temperature of the pen. Work your way from low temperature to higher temperature to see the results you get with each setting.

You can blur the tone between two contrasting tones to give yourself a practice run on the results you get with your burner and by changing the technique you will use.

The chapter reduces what is an otherwise complicated topic into a bite-sized chunk. It narrows down the many different types of information on pens and the craft of wood burning to absolute basics, defines the common categorizations used by brand developers, and gives details on how they lay the foundation for all pyrography pens and pen tips.

The more you understand your pens and pen tips, the better the results you will get with your wood burning craft. You will also be able to achieve smoother shading techniques with practice.

g) Shading Techniques

The emphasis on your shading techniques is practice. Take time to practice each technique methodically prior to dedicating time and effort to a design that requires a combination of many basic forms. Practice your line work, your circles, your dots, but most important, your shading technique. As your line work skill improves, your challenge will be to continuously do finer detailed line work, improving on your technique.

Once you are quite comfortable with line work and have done a number of complete projects to hone your ability, you may want to move on to more complex shading. As you get more comfortable with the feel of the wood burning pen in your hand and working on wood, take the next step and start finding a suitable design.

Using the shading techniques as a launch pad to how to use the pyrography pen, we show the reader how they can use basic art forms, namely, lines, circles, and other shapes, to add tone and depth to their work. The shading techniques discussed include contour lines, parallel line hatching, cross-hatching, and stippling, among others.

h) Design and pattern ideas

There is a lot that you can do with the pyrography pen. You have a wide variety of designs to pick from. Examples include nature, machinery, household equipment, festival and religious art, cartoons, and trending arts, just to name a few. Any of these images from these areas can be translated onto your piece of wood for a great wood burning experience. Take a deliberate approach when selecting images to use as designs. Choose designs that will enable you to practice the development of contour, tone, and texture in your work.

i) **Artistic Principles Used in Pyrography**

Artistic principles in pyrography are also found in other art forms. The pyrography artist will find points of harmony between what they are developing and what is happening in a lot of artwork they encounter. Such elements include contrast, balance, and visual tension.

As you continue to enhance your ideas of the materials you can use for pyrography, keep safety at the forefront of your mind. As you practice, you want to focus on knowing your pens and what each pen can do. Develop proficiency in how to make your lines, shapes, and always aim at mastering one skill before you go on to the next.

j) **Choosing and Applying a Finish**

Your pyrography art will last longer if you apply finish. Finish protects your work from regular wear and tear, weathering, and makes it sturdier. Finishes are in two main types; food-grade and chemical-based. Under the food-grade types, you can choose what to use for artworks that will be in contact with food and with human skin. On the list of chemical-based finishes, you will have a variety. What you want to focus on is a finish that will not alter your art significantly. Part of these considerations are finishes that add a hue to your final work.

Do you spray or paint? Always spray the first coat. Never paint if the artwork has an extra enhancement such as paint or color of any kind.

k) Troubleshooting

Do read the full chapter. Here are the issues discussed in the main text. You get to the market and the price tags are intimidating; what do you do? Why is your working area so smoky? My image transfer techniques need refining; what can I do? There is fine dust as I work, how can I clear it? Is your wood burner difficult to work with? We go through some things you might want to look at to solve these problems.

My lines are rough and jagged? My lines are too dark? The grain lines are interfering with my design work? My lines are bumpy along the wood grain? I can't seem to get the right tip to do what I want it to do? I lightened the pressure on my pen tip but I am still getting a bumpy burn? The final work has dents that shouldn't be there? I want to make a wider curve? Image transfer is still giving me difficulties?

My typography work is not going well, what can I do? My pen tips are black and have misshaped edges; what could be the problem? My pen tip broke inside my burner, what can I do? My burner is not working, why? We have studied solutions to all of these varying problems.

l) Mastering Self-expression Through Pyrography

Self-expression is the primary reason many of us take up a new art form. While tracing images directly is a good way to learn, there is more available to the budding enthusiast. Do not limit yourself to one method. Use modern technology such as computers to make repetitive tasks easier so that you can give all your attention to creating an individual art. Consider examples of other art down the centuries that can inspire you.

FINAL WORDS

You have come a long way since the beginning of this book. You have covered a lot of ground. Now all that remains is to put what you have learned into practice. There is no better way to refine any art skill than to practice the techniques that move ideas into the real world of accomplishment and attainment.

As you venture further into the pyrography art world, be courageous. Like all art forms, there are basic principles and when those are put into the individual presentation, they blossom into a unique and beautiful art. This is a wide open avenue to reveal the beautiful pieces stored within you. It is our hope that this book will inspire you to take wood burning beyond just being a hobby; we'd like to think that it will become part of your lifestyle.

Printed in Great Britain
by Amazon

71669753R00095